ove: 50050 *Fearless* & 50024 *Vanguard* haul 'The Fellsman II' railtour through Tebay on 23 April 1988.   **Neil Harvey**

st of the Last - The life & times of 50050 Fearless was edited d produced by Andy Coward, Ian Horner and Richard ompson for and on behalf of the D400 Fund.

e D400 Fund would like to express our grateful thanks to eryone who assisted in the publication of this book, in ticular the scores of photographers who made their images ely available for use and also to the people who have sisted with writing some of the chapters.

Acknowledgements to the photographers accompany each of the photographs and a full list of writers and photographer credits is contained at the back of this book.

All profits from the sale of this book will directly aid the ongoing restoration and maintenance of 50050 *Fearless*. More information about 50050 and the work done by the D400 Fund can be found by visiting ***www.d400fund.org.uk***, or you can contact us by e-mail to ***d400fund@d400fund.org.uk***.

Above: 50050 passes Dainton signalbox, working a Paddington to Penzance train on 23 September 1978. *Paul Winter*

© This book was produced by Andy Coward, Ian Horner and Richard Thompson
and is published by the D400 Fund. First published 2010.
ISBN No: 978-0-9566107-0-6

www.d400fund.org.uk

Front Cover: 50050 *Fearless* catches the weak early morning autumnal sun as it passes Lyneham on 18 October 1986 with the 1A1 07:00 Hereford - Paddington 'Cathedrals Express'. *Martin Loader*

Back Cover: D400 and 50033 *Glorious* pass through the Laira carriage washer with the empty coaching stock off the 1430 Meldon Plymouth charter service on 25 September 1993. *Peter Goodman*

Opposite Background: 50050 enters St Austell station whilst working the 1105 Penzance - Paddington on 1 June 1985. *John Maher*

First of the last

The life & times of 50050 *Fearless*

CONTENTS

Foreword

LES ROSS MBE - Broadcaster and Railway Enthusiast

I've never written a book foreword before, but I'll be 'fearless' (get it?) and press on. I suppose my qualification for doing this, is that I happen to be the owner of a locomotive - although it's not a Class 50. In fact, it's not even a diesel. One of the team involved in the production of this book - Richard Thompson - played a large part in the restoration of my Class 86 electric (86259 *Les Ross*). Well, he's turned his hand to reviving 50050 - and now, he, Andy Coward and Ian Horner have produced this "life story" of 50050 *Fearless*. Thank goodness for guys like them, that have the skills, knowledge and enthusiasm to keep these heritage locomotives alive.

I'm only a railway enthusiast who happens to have his own locomotive - it doesn't get much better than that. I know precious little of the technical side of things, but my life has been so enriched by just watching trains. You know - it's an emotion thing. It's only natural that we all have our favourite classes of locomotives, and sometimes our least favourite. But I've always noticed that, whatever those are, everyone seems to have a soft spot for a '50'. During their heydays, the Class 50s certainly worked all over the network, and from its early days as D400, *Fearless* was no exception, as this book will show.

In 1970, I began my radio career, and getting around on the railways began to take a back seat, but I do have one very vivid memory. Sometime in the early seventies, I spent a day on Carstairs station. I absolutely lapped up all those double-headed '50s' on the Euston to Glasgow trains. Oh, the eternal delight. A double-header. Two for the price of one. I don't think I realised at the time, that they ran double-headed to keep up with the fast-timed electrically-hauled part of the service, further south on the West Coast Main Line (Sorry, that's the last mention of electrics!). I thought the Class 50s were being put out two at a time as a treat for us spotters! I long ago lost my 1970s notebooks, so whether I saw D400 on that day, I don't know!

There are thousands of books on whole classes of locomotives, but very few about one locomotive, and we all know that every locomotive has its own individual personality - and a story to tell - so let Andy, Ian and Richard now tell you the story of the class pioneer 50050 *Fearless* - read on!

Steve Kemp

First of the last

Introduction

400 backs onto its train at Yeovil Junction
...tion on 12 January 1992.
...hn Chalcroft / www.railphotoprints.co.uk

The Class 50 locomotive needs little introduction to most British diesel enthusiasts. Nearly two decades on since British Rail finished with them, many continue to harbour strong views - both positive and negative - on this sometimes controversial and relatively small fleet of diesel locomotives.

Introduced just in time to help see off the last British Railways steam locomotives, the final 'mixed traffic' locomotive design (as opposed to specific traffic - freight or passenger), entered service in 1967. What should have been a high-tech thoroughly modern design suffered from poor reliability however, and the locomotives were judged difficult to work with in their early years based in the North West of England.

On completion of the West Coast Main Line electrification in 1974, the class gradually moved west and played a key role in the abandonment of much loved diesel hydraulic traction. The shallower grades of the Western Region allowed the class to better demonstrate its high speed credentials but reliability continued to be a problem.

Following naming in the late 1970s, a refurbishment programme to increase reliability and a bold new livery applied in the early 1980s, the class attracted new admirers. By the end of the 1980s and with locomotive hauled trains in decline, the class worked out its final years on the arduous Waterloo to Exeter route.

With little money left to be spent on the class, reliability again suffered and for many locomotives the end came almost as a blessed relief. For the final two years before British Rail was privatised in 1994, three locomotives were kept back to work a number of railtours to destinations old and new, ensuring the class finished its career in some style.

The first built locomotive of the fleet - D400, or 50050 as many knew it, and later named *Fearless* - was present throughout the whole 27 years of Class 50 operations for British Rail. More than 16 years after it was retired by BR, 50050 has also had a varied and interesting history in preservation. This then is *First of the Last* - the story of one locomotive, told in the context of the life and times of the complete fleet of 50 Class 50s.

The life & times of 50050 *Fearless*

DP2 stands at King's Cross station whil working services on the ECML.
Ivan Stewart Collectio

Marrying the proven and reliable English Electric 16-cylinder engine with a 'Deltic' bodyshell led to EE's DP2 trial locomotive, which proved to be such a success that it led to the Class 50 order. **MARK HICKEN** looks back at the locomotive's life.

In the early 1960s, the English Electric Company (EE) was involved in various manufacturing projects, including the building of 22 Napier-engined Type 5 'Deltic' locomotives for British Railways (BR), and the development of new engines for a number of overseas customers.

The upshot of this situation was the sidelining of the SVT range of engines, which had first seen use in H Ivatt's pioneering LMS diesel-electric 10000, and subsequently in improved and up-rated form in the Modernisation Plan EE Type 4s.

Thus, when the British Transport Commission announced its desire for a new generation of higher powered diesels in January 1960, the company was not in the best position to take up the challenge,

especially in comparison with rivals Sulzer which had continued to advance its LDA engine. The Swiss firm was already well ahead in the power stakes with its 2,500hp 12LDA28-B (as fitted to the production Class 45s), while EE was still only able to offer the same 2,000hp 16SVT unit that powered the Class 40s.

Clearly a huge increase in power and performance was required, and quickly, if the company stood any chance of competing for orders. Unfortunately the new engines developed for export were not sufficiently proven, leaving the option of trying to boost the power of the SVT engine without exceeding the existing thermal and mechanical stress limits of the design.

It was decided to build a pressure-charged, inter-cooled

variant of the tried and tested 16-cylinder unit, to raise power output to 2,700hp. To improve pressure at higher speeds and give increased throughput of air and greater fuelling, whilst also controlling temperatures to avoid damage to the blowers and exhaust manifolds, four turbochargers were required as opposed to the single device used in Sulzer's LDA.

The engine in this form was offered to the BTC, but the sheer scale of the uprating from 2,000 to 2,700hp was considered a major risk, and although similar configurations had been tried with some success abroad, BR insisted the unit be put through a workout in a mobile testbed.

Given the urgency involved, EE opted to utilise one of the already fabricated 'Deltic' bodyshells and bogie sets available at its Vulcan Works in Newton-le-Willows, and simply place in the 16CSVT engine. Fortunately this was possible without major modification - the most obvious external differences being the large bodyside radiator grilles and the single roof-mounted fan.

The medium-speed 850rpm engine was coupled with an EE 840/1B main generator and auxiliary EE 911/5C unit, while six axle-hung, nose-suspended EE 538A traction motors provided power to the wheels. A Clayton steam heat boiler was fitted against the Commission's desire for Electric Train Supply, while light alloy material was used for the fuel and boiler water tanks which were beneath the underframe.

In the spring of 1962, Vulcan Foundry job D733 was completed and while several different suggestions were made, no accord could be found with regard to a name, so the rather perfunctory DP2 - for Diesel Prototype 2 - was adopted. The finished article, painted in a coat of dark Brunswick green complete with the now obligatory yellow warning panels, was a simple and robust machine which weighed 105 tons and had an axle-load of a mere 17.5 tons, resulting in a power to weight ratio similar to that of the diesel-hydraulics.

DP2 travelled light from Vulcan Works to Chester and back on 2 May 1962, followed by a 15-coach trial run between Crewe and Penrith on the 8th. During these early days general maintenance was split between the manufacturer and BR, EE engineering staff usually riding on the footplate, although in light of the locomotive's exceptional reliability this practice became increasingly unnecessary.

On 14 May, DP2 began its initial loan period with BR on regular London Midland Region trains from Euston to Liverpool, later extended to Blackpool, and it was during this time a premature demise almost befell the locomotive whilst visiting the new diesel depot at Camden five days later on 19 May.

For ease of maintenance, the running rails at the depot were raised about three feet above ground level - unfortunately when DP2 ran onto them, the supports buckled under the weight and the locomotive was left hanging precariously over the inspection pit. Fortunately, the only slight damage sustained was to the No. 1 end bogie frame.

After repairs and adjustments, work was resumed on the West Coast Main Line (WCML) where one of its few failures occurred, albeit in the extenuating circumstances of the extreme blizzard conditions of January 1963, when after much slow running and several signal checks, the radiators froze.

These WCML duties were soon recognised as inappropriate for two reasons. Firstly, there was a question mark regarding the applicability of testing a diesel electric on a route undergoing electrification, and secondly, the schedules undertaken were those more typically associated with Type 4 2,000hp locomotives, and thus, like D0280 *Falcon*, DP2 was rarely extended.

Following an engine inspection and the replacement of the boiler in June 1963, the locomotive duly moved to the Eastern Region, based at Finsbury Park to work alongside the 'Deltics'. Here on the demanding East Coast Main Line (ECML) King's Cross to 'Edinburgh diagram DP2 was finally able to show its paces by 'substituting for the 3,300hp Type 5s, which were themselves taking turns out of traffic to have their boilers modified. Even in the exacting environment, where full power was required over long distances, the Type 4 managed to keep to the schedules with relative ease, sometimes bettering them, in a period of almost two months consistently trouble-free running.

The autumn of 1963 saw the locomotive at Stephenson and Hawthorn's Darlington plant to have its bogies swapped for a modified design similar to those used on the new EE Type 3 diesels then appearing on the Western Region (WR). There followed a major overhaul in April 1965 after 360,000 miles when strengthening

The most obvious physical differences between DP2 and the Deltics were the large radiator grilles, as seen behind the cab door in this view of DP2 at Peterborough in August 1964. *Grahame Wareham*

work on the crankshaft was undertaken along with new turbocharger air-intakes, the locomotive emerging to take charge of the 'Master Cutler' in full 'Deltic' livery. By this time BR had agreed to rent DP2 at 12.5p/mile which EE hoped would ultimately cover its manufacturing costs.

In 1962, long before any significant conclusions could be drawn from the Type 4 prototypes - indeed only just after the introduction of DP2 - BR had already ordered a small batch of new 2,750hp mixed-traffic locomotives from Brush, using electrical equipment and uprated versions of engines originally destined for the final 20 Class 46 Peaks. These Brush Type 4s proved troublesome in their early years, so the British Railways Board - which had superseded the BTC in January 1963 - had considered ordering 50 DP2s to accelerate schedules on the non-electrified portion of the WCML.

This idea was dropped in favour of a series of far more complicated machines based substantially on the prototype, but incorporating a sophisticated package of electronics, elements of which were fitted into DP2 in January 1966 for initial testing. The locomotives built in 1967/68 were the Class 50s, numbered D400-D449, which were leased by BR, and intended as a stop-gap measure to speed up services between Crewe and Glasgow, where they were regularly deployed in pairs.

The 2,700hp Class 50s used a similar engine and main generator to DP2, but incorporated many experimental control systems, such as automatic tractive effort and slow speed control, as well as dual brakes and Electric Train Supply, in a new flat-fronted design. After early teething troubles associated with their complexity, they were transferred to the WR where they replaced the Class 52s on West of England expresses with considerable success.

DP2 continued on a variety of duties for the next 18 months, when in summer 1967 tragedy struck. While deputising for a 'Deltic' on the noon King's Cross to Edinburgh run on 31 July, DP2 was heading north at speed near Thirsk, when the train crew noticed a strange haze in the near distance. It transpired that a goods train of 'Cemflo' cement wagons travelling in the same direction on the adjacent slow line had partially derailed leaving one wagon fouling the main line. Driver Evans made an emergency brake application but it was too late, the express ploughed into the stray cement wagon at around 50mph resulting in the derailment of the locomotive and the leading seven carriages. Sadly seven passengers were killed.

Although the train remained upright, the impact was severe enough to cause serious damage to the locomotive's No. 1 end, resulting in buckled frames. In such condition DP2 was deemed uneconomic for repair, so the engine was removed for use in the '50s' and the bodyshell was broken up in October 1968.

For five years DP2 had proved the most successful of the next generation Type 4 diesel electric prototypes, achieving better than 125,000 service miles per year, 627,000 in total, whilst suffering remarkably few failures. EE must have been optimistic of a positive response from BR, but the resulting order for just 50 Type 4s based on the project would have been a huge disappointment to the company's board.

This article originally appeared in the June 2010 issue of Railways Illustrated magazine and it is reproduced here by kind permission of both the author and Railways Illustrated Editor Pip Dunn.

Another view of English Electric's Type 4 prototype locomotive DP2 standing on the blocks at Kings Cross station in this undated photograph.
Grahame Wareham

Chapter 2
A New Dawn

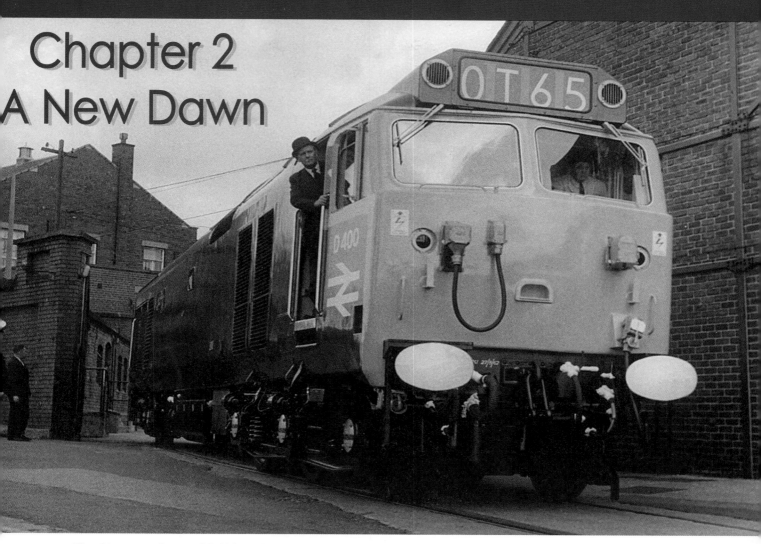

The historic roll-out of D400, with the locomotive emerging through the works gates of Vulcan Foundry in Newton-le-Willows, in June 1967. Leaning out of the cab is London Midland Region Chief Traction Inspector John Hughes, whilst LMR Chief Driving Instructor Arnold Amson is at the controls as D400 makes its first moves following completion.
Eddie Bellass

In late summer 1967 another rather anonymous diesel-electric locomotive rolled off the production line ready for service with British Rail (BR). Of course, each and every newly built locomotive starts its life as just a series of numbers. Some however, may through the course of their working life become more than that - albeit to relatively few people outside those who work for or enjoy their interest in "the railway".

BR's latest and indeed final mixed traffic design - the 'D400' Class comprised just 50 locomotives of which Works No. D1141 and the English Electric Company No. 3770 was the first to be built. BR christened its latest acquisition D400 and accepted it into service on October 3 1967 -

ready for a career that would span 27 years.

The English Electric Company (EE) was extremely proud of its new design with its advanced features not previously seen on diesel locomotives. The front page of the September 1967 edition of *Modern Railways* magazine, which read like an advertisement featured a photograph of the yet to be painted D400. The accompanying text drew attention to its modern features proclaiming the new locomotives as; the world's first diesel-electrics with automatic tractive effort control, automatic slow speed control and automatic integrated brake control. This was balanced by confirmation that the design was based on the highly regarded prototype locomotive DP2, which had given excellent

service until its untimely demise in summer 1967.

In addition however, as confidence in its own locomotive design expertise grew, BR insisted on a host of additional equipment and systems - much of which had not been tested anywhere. All this led to the new machines being much more complex than DP2, which beyond the main power equipment and some of the running gear were to all intents

The replica English Electric builders plate fitted to D400 following its retro-repaint in 1991.
Martin Loader

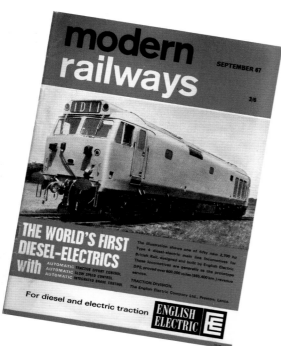

modern railways

SEPTEMBER 67

3/6

THE WORLD'S FIRST DIESEL-ELECTRICS with
AUTOMATIC TRACTIVE EFFORT CONTROL
AUTOMATIC LOW SPEED CONTROL
AUTOMATIC INTEGRATED BRAKE CONTROL

The illustration shows one of fifty new 2,700 hp
Type 4 diesel-electric main line locomotives for
British Rail, designed and built by English Electric.
These locomotives are generally as the prototype
DP2, proved over 600,000 miles (965,400 km.) revenue
service.

TRACTION DIVISION,
The English Electric Company Ltd., Preston, Lancs.

For diesel and electric traction **ENGLISH ELECTRIC** E

and purposes brand new. If the London Midland Region (LMR) operators - who would be taking on the new locomotives - were expecting 50 clones of the fondly remembered DP2 to enter service, they would be mistaken.

Built at Vulcan Foundry, near Earlestown in Lancashire, D400 moved to its initial base at Crewe diesel depot on 11 September for allocation to LMR Western Lines duties. The next day it made two return trips to Stafford hauling 15 coaches, attaining 100 mph in the process. Two days later on the 13th it was heavy freight for the new locomotive with a 1,000 ton oil train from Stanlow to Dalmarnock near Glasgow providing a stiff test on the gradients of Shap and Beattock.

On 15 September another freight train was hauled, this time from Bamfurlong Sidings near Wigan to Hellifield and back - a duty repeated five days later. These early trials were considered successful by both BR and EE, although as would be expected a number of minor niggles emerged. On 22 September, D400 returned to Vulcan Works for rectification of these issues.

The locomotive was returned to Crewe by the end of the month

and after another heavily loaded trial in early October, EE delivered its final commissioning report. BR then issued an acceptance certificate and D400 retired to Crewe depot for a B-exam before being made available for crew training. By the end of 1967, three more '400' Class locomotives had been accepted to traffic; D401/D402/D404 - the missing D403 was not accepted until mid January 1968 and followed D405 into service. The 50th and last of the fleet to be accepted, D449 (now officially known as 449), finally entered service in December 1968. All were painted in corporate blue livery with full yellow ends extending back round the cab-side windows.

BR managed to acquire the fleet of 50 locomotives cheaply by taking them on a leasing agreement with EE. In addition to the usual manufacturer's 'guarantee' for new equipment, EE agreed to guarantee that 84% of the class would be available for service at 09.00 each day. Any shortfall not caused by BR would be subject to a penalty. This financial arrangement suited both parties, especially BR at a time when government investment in the railways did not always match what was required. That said, had

sufficient funds been made available for full electrification of the West Coast Main Line (WCML) beyond Weaver Junction, then the '400' Class locomotives would probably have not been ordered at all. All 50 locomotives carried a small plate on each bodyside confirming ownership by EE until BR bought the fleet outright in the mid 1970s.

On entering service, the new locomotives were put to work on a variety of passenger and freight train duties centred on the north west of England. Primarily working trains hitherto handled by '1500' Class locomotives (later Class 47), the '400s' became a daily sight on the WCML north of Crewe, as well as on Merseyside and in the Manchester area. Spare capacity also allowed the new machines to replace '200' Class locomotives (later Class 40) on some secondary workings. The '400s' also appeared at Perth after working an overnight sleeper service, which led to other wanderings around Scotland, including Edinburgh. For further reading on the early years in particular, the reader is recommended to refer to the excellent book *Class 50s in Operation* by David N Clough.

D400 is shunted around Vulcan Foundry Works by D8319 in September 1967. It had returned for rectification works, following its initial operating trials. *John Chalcroft / www.railphotoprints.co.uk*

On 18 May 1969 the first major incident involving a '400' occurred when D417 slipped to a stand on Beattock Bank while heading the 1S07 21.30 Euston - Inverness. The train immediately behind, the 1S18 22.15 Euston - Glasgow, which was being hauled by D400, was initially commandeered to provide rear end assistance but the driver of D417 managed to restart his train. The driver of D400 then ran heavily into the rear of the Inverness train, with fatal consequences. D400 sustained extensive damage to its No.1 cab in the collision and was immediately despatched to Crewe Works. Repairs took some time to carry out and while it was in works, the bogies and power unit were taken for re-use on other locomotives in the fleet. 400 finally emerged in late January 1970, but made a brief return to Crewe in early February for rectification work on its new power unit.

Above: An immaculate D400 is displayed at an open day at Crewe in November 1967. Behind the locomotive is second-built D401.
Grahame Wareham

In late June and early July 1968, industrial action by signallers saw many Anglo-Scottish services diverted to Edinburgh via the Waverley route. D416 seems to have been the first '400' on the long-closed line when it worked through with the 12.05 from Euston on 28 June, with D400 making an appearance a few days later on 3 July. Ten days later, D400 made the class debut on an ordinary service train at Glasgow Queen Street when it worked the 13.10 to Aberdeen as far as Perth at least.

A major working soon after re-entering normal service was haulage of the 16.10 Glasgow - Euston throughout on 18 March.

Below: A brand new D400 passes Ais Gill on the Settle and Carlisle route with an early test run in September 1967. D400 would be accepted into traffic the following month. *George Woods*

The life & times of 50050 *Fearless*

This was apparently due to industrial action by staff at Crewe South Signal Box, and the train ran via Manchester.

In 1970, the first classified repairs for the '400' Class were completed at Crewe Works with the re-introduction to traffic of 415 in mid January following a light overhaul. 400 did not receive the call for its light overhaul until November 1971 and was the 49th to be so treated. It may seem surprising that the doyen of the class would be so far down the shopping order, but this does not take into account the long period inside Crewe Works following the Beattock collision. 400 did, of course, return to traffic with a new power unit - helping to see it through to shopping time the following year. For the record, the light overhaul program was completed with the release of 426 in January 1972.

The highlight of the May 1970 timetable change on the WCML was the start of the accelerated timings facilitated by the use of '400s' in pairs north of Crewe. Most Euston trains were booked double-headers, along with those running to and from Birmingham. In addition, the Liverpool/Manchester to Glasgow combined services featured a pair of '400s' throughout from Merseyside. From July 1973, many trains changed from electric to diesel traction at Preston.

The 48 locomotives introduced without multiple-working jumper connections on their cab fronts (all except 400 and 401) were fitted with the equipment in time for the new timetable, commencing on Monday 4 May. This permitted up to three '400s' to be operated simultaneously with one driver - the connections were unique to the class and marked by an orange square symbol above each buffer. On the first day of the speeded up services, the down 'Royal Scot' was powered north of Crewe by 437 and 447 with a commemorative headboard carried by the lead locomotive.

As a taste of performance exploits to come over the next few years, the pair covered the "trial section" between Carnforth and Shap summit at a previously unheard of average speed of 84.7mph.

Haulage of such high-profile express passenger trains contrasted with the regular freight workings taken by the class, often loose coupled and running via the Settle and Carlisle line.

News coverage of the '400' Class, or Class 50s as they would soon be known, in the railway press in the 1970s was scarce - in spite of a reputation for poor reliability which surely would have been worth a few reports? The class featured regularly however, in the long running Railway Practice and Performance features published in The Railway Magazine. Detailed timing logs of trains hauled by the '400s' were accompanied by high praise from the celebrated train timer Mr O S Nock as some fantastic performances were put up,

400 awaits departure from Larbert with 1S53 08.3? Birmingham New Street Perth on 24 February 197? shortly after it re-entere? traffic after collision repairs.
Jim Binn?

First of the last

400 basks in the sun as it pauses at Preston with the 5J42 van train in this undated view of the locomotive from the early 1970's. *Ivan Stewart Collection*

particularly on the gradients of the WCML. One such article featured 413 and 404 whipping 12 coaches weighing in at 420 tons, from Carnforth to Shap summit at an exhilarating average speed of 88mph. This run, just like the inaugural official double-header, exceeded the line speed at the top of the climb by 8mph.

GEC

2700hp
DIESEL ELECTRICS FOR BRITISH RAIL
CLASS 50
GEC Traction Limited

By 1970, the 'D' prefix had been removed from most diesel locomotives and, as such, 400 stands at Carlisle with service 1M24 on 4 April 1970.

John Chalcroft / www.railphotoprints.co.uk

The early years of the Class 50s

Main image above: The old order and the new at Lostock Hall on 30 May 1968, as an almost brand new D417 works an express passenger service through Farrington Junction, whilst Stanier 8F 2-8-0 steam locomotives 48765 and 48730 shunt in the sidings - within three months steam traction on the British Railways network would have been eliminated.

Inset above: D415 and D416 head a northbound express service at the same location, but looking in the opposite direction. Lostock Hall engine shed was located just off the right hand side of the picture in the distance.

Both: Terry Campbell

Below Left: D401 heads a West Coast Main Line service into Preston station, passing beneath the station's impressive signal gantry in 1969.

Ivan Stewart Collection

Below Right: D402 in charge of 1S25 2230 London Euston - Perth sleeper near Bonnymuir on 14 July 1971.

Jim Binnie

First of the last

Above: The railways in and around Wigan were also good places to spot English Electric Type 4 locomotives. D404 speeds past Wigan Springs Branch depot in the early 1970s with a down express.

Above Right: A view of the interior of Wigan Springs Branch depot in the early 1970s, with D437 rubbing shoulders with a wide variety of traction, including Class 85 E3065, three Class 40s and a pair Class 25s.

Right: D439 heads a goods train through Wigan North Western, whilst to the left of the picture can be seen evidence of station modernisation works getting underway.

Below: An up express speeds along the WCML towards Wigan North Western, as viewed from the delightful neighbouring Wigan Wallgate. The signage and station furniture provides a real glimpse back to the past.

All: Ivan Stewart Collection

The life & times of *50050 Fearless*

Chapter 3
Going West

As funds were made available for full electrification to Glasgow, it became clear the LMR would soon no longer need the '400s' - certainly not in current numbers anyway. The British Railways National Traction Plan published in the late 1960s had signalled the phasing out of the Western Region (WR) diesel-hydraulic locomotives and the future availability of the '400s' had been noted. In October 1972, with the introduction of the Class 87 electric locomotive not far away, 400 was sent to Bristol Bath Road depot for crew training, working to Taunton and back on 19 October for familiarisation of local traction inspectors.

On 25 November, 400 visited its future home of Old Oak Common depot and five days later worked down to Plymouth. On 1 December it visited Paddington station for the first time - it was apparently Paddington staff that

coined the nickname 'Hoover' on account of the sound made by air passing through the inertial-filter fins. The first use on a scheduled service on the WR occurred on 15 January 1973 when 400 worked the 17.12 Paddington - Weston Super Mare. In August it was allocated to a Bristol to Weymouth excursion train but failed on the outward trip at Maiden Newton.

Later in 1973, 401 and 402 followed 400 from Crewe to Bristol, triggering the onward movement of 400 to Laira depot to start crew training - although it remained allocated to Bristol. Over the next few months the locomotive was used to train South Western drivers ahead of a planned mass entry to service from May 1974. Scheduled exams were still carried out at Bristol Bath Road and it would occasionally be swapped with 401 to facilitate maintenance. On 22

November 1973 Class 25, 5230 hauling the 08.00 Bristol - Penzance failed at Exeter. Assistance to Plymouth was provided by 400 - the first time a '400' hauled a passenger train in Devon.

In early 1974, 400 returned to Laira with a new identity - 50050, following renumbering in accordance with the new TOPS system at Bath Road depot on 27 February. Now officially known as Class 50s and recorded as 50xxx, renumbering was achieved by taking the last two digits from the original number and placing in a series beginning with 50001. First built 400 took the new number of 50050 as each series would start with a one rather than a zero.

The introduction of the interlopers in the west was far from smooth. Engineers at Laira depot, happy and content with their diesel-hydraulics, were not

50050 near Somerton with a Kensington to St Austell Motorail service on 20 May 1978. 50050 was identifiable amongst the Class 50 fleet, as it was the only one not to have grab handles fitted beneath the windscreens on the cab fronts. *John Chalcroft / www.railphotoprints.co.uk*

easily convinced that these new diesel-electrics would be the trouble free, easily maintainable locomotives that management said they would be. Unofficially rumours spread that the LMR had been only too pleased to be getting rid of them. The interiors were filthy and the numerous internal doors were not popular with fitters crawling round the locomotives. The advanced electronics were well beyond the experience of men used to working on Class 25s and 46s - especially the electronic control systems, but also the sub systems for slow speed control, current limiting and rheostatic braking.

To help ease the learning curve, the Chief Mechanical and Electrical Engineer sent his own representatives down to Devon. Some fitting staff, convinced that drivers were being trained ahead of the engineers, simply avoided the interlopers and stuck with the hydraulics. Anecdotal evidence suggests many drivers didn't get the chance to learn Class 50s because so few of them were actually in service. In April 1974 the renumbered 50003 was officially reallocated to Laira - the start of an association that would span 20 years. The first job was the completion of a D-exam but continuing unfamiliarity, general apathy and the need to order all spares from Bristol combined to make for a long drawn out job.

Back on the LMR, the May 1974 timetable heralded the official launch of electrified services throughout from Euston to Glasgow Central resulting in more Class 50s looking for new duties. A re-shuffle of the fleet saw all but 12 locomotives transferred to the WR, but a fortnight later three were returned to Crewe - perhaps the class wasn't so unloved after all? At the same time 50050 along with 50001/002/004/005 became the first Class 50s to be allocated to Old Oak Common depot - beginning a 16 year association with the London depot.

In February 1975, 50050 entered Crewe Works for the final time to receive its second classified repair - an intermediate overhaul. The locomotive remained in Works for almost three months before returning to traffic on the WR in mid-May. Remarkably, it had retained the same place in the shopping order (49th) after its light overhaul 39 months earlier. By this time, some Class 50s at the

The railway line close to Bath features some impressive tunnels and structures, including the tunnels at Twerton, with their castle-style entrance construction giving them a distinctive appearance. 50050 heads through the shorter Twerton Tunnel with a diverted Plymouth to London Paddington train.
John Chalcroft / www.railphotoprints.co.uk

The life & times of 50050 *Fearless*

Just over a month before naming, 50050 heads towards Lostwithiel on 17 July 1978 with a Penzance to Paddington express. *Brian Morrison*

head of the order had received their third classified repair (another light overhaul); including 50050's Old Oak shed-mate 50004, which now led the overhaul cycle. From December 1976, Doncaster Works took over responsibility for Class 50 repairs and completed its first overhaul, for 50009, in June 1977.

From October 1975, the last of the Class 52 'Western' diesel-hydraulic locomotives were supposed to have moved onto freight duties, leaving the way clear for their successors to take over. Slightly better availability of Class 50s during the summer had helped sideline seven more Class 52s, but the WR was canny enough to continue to maintain the train heating boilers of the survivors - a good thing too as Class 52s continued to be required for passenger work until their final demise in early 1977. On 3 October, 50050 teamed up with Class 52 1022 to work the 23.15 Paddington - Oxford. This turn was often by used by Old Oak Common depot to test a locomotive after being stopped for repairs.

In April 1976, 50050 moved west to Laira depot - its home for all but seven months of the next 18

years. From the May 1976 timetable change, the remaining LMR based Class 50s joined the rest of the fleet on the Western. Duties at this time were primarily the haulage of Paddington to Bristol express passenger trains and similar services to and from the south west. These were supplemented by turns to Birmingham from both Paddington and Plymouth, although the Devon workings often changed locomotives at Gloucester. Summer duties took the class to Newquay and for a short while, Falmouth also.

In the long hot summer of 1976, 50050 made two visits to Falmouth working in on the 08.22 from Truro before taking holidaymakers home on the 09.10 Falmouth - Paddington. During this year, BR officially abandoned the practice of displaying train reporting numbers (head-codes) on locomotive front ends. Most had their blinds wound round to show 0O00 but on the WR certain variations were noted. Some had the leading zero wound down to show 'one' in order to read 1O00 in tribute to the much lamented hydraulic traction. Others displayed a version of the locomotive's number - in 50050's case this showed 5O50. The latter

variation, applied to several Class 50s was the work of the same member of staff at Laira depot - so the story goes! The winding gear was later replaced by a pair of lights set behind a plate of blackened glass. Two white dots in the glass gave the appearance of a 'double one' domino above the windscreens. Laira depot carried out this modification to 50050 sometime around 1976/77.

The early years of work on the WR were marked by even worse reliability than on the London Midland, much to the delight of the class's many detractors. When first transferred, the LMR offered technical assistance to the WR, which was politely refused. This was perhaps unwise considering the complicated box of tricks being inherited. Interestingly the 15 Class 50s still allocated to Crewe, began to show marked improvements in reliability now that they were used on more diverse and less intensive duties than previously. In the latter half of 1975 and into 1976 the Crewe machines achieved a reliability figure of over 26,000 miles per casualty (failure) and an availability of 77%. The WR-based fleet could only manage 9,250 miles and 58%. Since the introduction of the new Inter-City 125 trains on the WR, a failed Class 50 could potentially cause even more disruption as the train immediately behind was often incapable of propelling it out of the way.

Such poor levels of reliability could not be sustained, particularly as the Class 50s now formed such an integral element of the WR's passenger train locomotive fleet. Plans were first hatched during 1977 for a partial rebuild of the fleet to address the known weak areas. Reliability did improve, thanks to the isolation of some of the electrical equipment which was deemed surplus to requirements by the locomotives' new keepers. 1978 figures of

Exeter regularly played host to the Class 50s throughout their career on the Western Region, where 50050 pulls away beneath the wonderful signal gantry on 30 July 1977. *John Chalcroft / www.railphotoprints.co.uk*

8,314 miles per casualty and 63% availability however, were still just not good enough. Such frailties might invite the question, why continue with the Class 50s? Perhaps the answer is that they consistently showed the virtues promised; the ability to run fast, work hard and deliver high mileages on express passenger work. Even in 1977, the fleet delivered on average 104,000 miles each against the BR average of 56,000. That kind of productivity would always allow shortcomings elsewhere to be viewed sympathetically.

The British Railways Board eventually agreed to a general overhaul or refurbishment programme for the class, which would completely strip and rebuild the interior of each locomotive. Unfortunately, funding did not cover the replacement of the main generator in favour of an alternator - a decision

ultimately proven as myopic.

The first locomotive to be selected for general overhaul was 50006, which had entered Doncaster Works in September 1977 for main generator repairs. Initially no work was carried out and the locomotive languished in works throughout 1978 awaiting materials. This in itself was not unusual as Doncaster had more than enough work on and Class 55s always took priority - but this did nothing for the reputation of the Class 50s.

At the turn of 1979 the repair was reclassified as a general overhaul, but progress was inevitably slow as 50006 was used as a guinea pig for new designs and ideas hatched by the Railway Technical Centre at Derby. During its sojourn, other Class 50s passed through the works for intermediate overhauls - effectively overtaking 50006 which seemed in danger

of becoming the forgotten Class 50.

From 1978 onwards, BR started applying names to the Class 50s. This began on 17 January, when the name *Ark Royal* was unveiled on the flanks of 50035 at Plymouth station by Captain Anson of the Royal Navy aircraft carrier bearing the same name. A pair of replica crests fitted above the nameplates further embellished the locomotive. By the end of 1979, all 50 locomotives carried the names of Royal Navy warships or shore establishments, in an order carefully chosen to keep vessels grouped by type and historical era. All but a handful of names were applied without ceremony at Laira depot as and when locomotives came on shed for exams and repairs.

On 4 August 1978, Laira depot christened 50050 *Fearless* only to

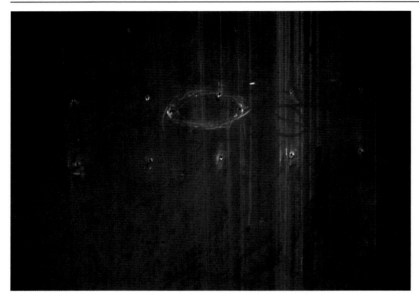

This anonymous photo showing the bodyside of 50050 was taken in August 1978, with evidence that the *Fearless* nameplates had been fitted and then temporarily removed, prior to the official naming ceremony and twinning with HMS Fearless on 23 August. The photo also shows the outline of the former English Electric Leasing Plate. **Alex Bayliss**

remove the nameplates three days later. This was because the Royal Navy having previously declined the invitation to take part in an official naming ceremony changed its mind. The nameplates were re-fixed in time for a ceremony at Laira depot on 23 August when Captain Thomas presented large patterned replicas of the ship's crest made of gun metal to be carried above each nameplate. The then H.M.S. Fearless was an assault ship of 12,120 tons displacement built in Belfast by Harland & Wolff and launched at the end 1963. The vessel later played a crucial role in the retaking of the Falkland Islands in 1982. This was the eighth ship to carry the name, previous incarnations dated back to the late 18th century - while back in the 20th, 50050 became the 43rd Class 50 to carry a name.

In between its two 'namings' *Fearless* could be observed in traffic with ten holes in each flank - where the nameplates had been removed. Somebody helpfully reminded observers of the locomotive's intended name by scrawling "Fearless" in the dirt inside the neat rows of holes! Following the official ceremony there was little dirt to be seen as the spruced up 50050 looked a fine sight, proudly displaying its newly applied 'bling'.

Over the first weekend of September, 50050 worked the Kensington Olympia to St Austell motor-rail service on Saturday and Sunday before taking the down 'Golden Hind' from Paddington on Monday evening 4 September. The summer timetable ended four weeks later with 50050 working the Saturday morning Newquay to Paddington service. In November, the locomotive spent a couple of days working with 50020 *Revenge* as the pair handled the 1M60 15.15 Plymouth - Manchester as far as Gloucester on 17 November. The next day the duo

worked the 08.05 Bristol - Penzance. An unusual duty brought 50050 to Cardiff Central on Saturday 16 December, when it arrived with the 11.20 from Hereford, formed of an air-conditioned rake of coaches presumably off one of the Paddington departures on Friday night.

Over a decade into their careers, Class 50s had rarely been requested traction for railtours - let's face it they hadn't been very popular! After the fleet had received names however, they attracted much more attention from enthusiasts - especially those too young to have experienced the diesel-hydraulics. In March 1978, named Class 50s had been requested for a Railway Pictorial Publishing Railtours (RPPR) tour from Paddington to various locations in the Midlands and the WR obliged with 50010 *Monarch* and 50048 *Dauntless*.

Three months later, 50016 *Barham* worked the Paddington to Birmingham leg of a trip to Doncaster Works. On 10 March 1979 the DAA Railtour Society (Daft as Anything - or something like that) organised a charter train from London to York via a circuitous route with haulage by English Electric traction. Starting from London Bridge station, 50050 took charge of the 'The West Riding Limited' trip running via Ipswich and Spalding to Healey Mills, where two Class 37s were provided for the short run on to York. After taking fuel at Healey Mills depot, the Class 50 followed

Opposite: In a time when the Class 50 fleet was often covered in a layer of grime and dirt, a relatively clean 50050 *Fearless* stands at London Waterloo on 6 October 1980. **Paul Winter**
Left: A close-up study of the *Fearless* nameplate and large HMS Fearless ships badge which were unveiled on 50050 on 23 August 1978. **John Mahon**

light diesel to York before returning the train to London Victoria via Selby and a swift run up the ECML. This is thought to be the only time a Class 50 traversed the now-closed March to Spalding route under its own power.

In mid June 1979, Old Oak Common depot exchanged the bogies from 50050 and 50035 so as to put the better set underneath 50035. Four years on from its intermediate overhaul at Crewe Works, 50050 had reached shopping time again and it was decided to take 50035's worn bogies away at the same time.

Entering Doncaster Works for the first time in late June, 50050 was earmarked for an intermediate overhaul even though the locomotive shopped ahead of it (50017 *Royal Oak*) would be given a general overhaul (refurbishment). In the infant days of the refurbishment project some Class 50s continued to be given a

standard intermediate overhaul because of the shorter turn round time. This practice kept a steady flow of locomotives coming back into traffic while lessons learned with locomotives at the front end of the refurbishment programme were used to reduce the time on works for the later rebuilds. After 50050 had been shopped, the next in line - 50027 *Lion* - was given an intermediate while the one after that - 50019 *Ramillies* - took its place in the refurbishment line.

Doncaster Works continued to carry out intermediate overhauls on unrefurbished Class 50s until 50030 *Repulse* went on its way in the middle of September 1980 - after spending less than three months in works. The next outshopped refurbished '50' - 50004 *St Vincent* - had been out of service for twice as long. On completion of its intermediate overhaul, 50050 returned to service in mid December 1979 being noted hauling the 4B10 Bristol - Plymouth vans one week

before Christmas and the 15.30 Paddington - Penzance on Christmas Eve. On New Year's Day it was back at Paddington, with a thin layer of winter grime already starting to blight the new paintwork!

While 50050 had been away at Doncaster, the first locomotive hauled trains on the Paddington to the West of England route had been taken over by the new Inter-City 125 trains (usually known as the High Speed Train, or HST). Three up/down Penzance and one up/down Plymouth jobs were switched straight away with others to follow during the period to the May 1980 timetable change. The fastest journey time from Paddington to Penzance now fell to just five hours and eight minutes.

Daily performance of Class 50s continued to interest the railway press and its correspondents. Some of the monthlies published regional traffic reports, many of

which focussed on locomotive failures. The Western reports often read badly - with Class 50s inevitably featuring in reports of failed trains and heavy delays. A letter printed in *Modern Railways* magazine complained about unfair reporting and suggested that reports of Class 50 failures were written with an underlying negative attitude to the fleet in general. The traffic report in the same issue listed only one locomotive failure by painted number - 50014 *Warspite*, but the locomotive (not a Class 50) hauling a freight train which failed on Beattock before rolling backwards to collide with the train behind remained anonymous. The correspondent may have had a point!

Most reports in the early months of 1980 confirmed 50050 sticking to its staple diet of West of England services to and from London Paddington, including the 08.08 Paddington - Plymouth diverted via Melksham on Sunday

27 January. Trips to Gloucester or Birmingham New Street from Plymouth also remained common. From the May timetable change, there was a major development as Class 50s began daily service on the Exeter to Waterloo line, taking over from Class 33s. As more and more HSTs entered service, higher powered passenger train locomotives such as Classes 47, 50 and 55 found themselves displaced from top jobs and forced to seek alternative work.

Driver training had started the previous November, with a Class 50 from Laira depot being used on the 06.15 Exeter - Waterloo and 13.00 Waterloo - Exeter services. This turn produced 50050 in mid-April. The full service, requiring six locomotives per day, commenced on 12 May, with the extra power available being exploited to reduce journey times and increase loadings by an extra coach. 50050 worked the line in the first week of the new timetable, being noted arriving at

Exeter with the 13.10 from Waterloo on 17 May.

In summer 1980 Class 50s made a limited return to the Paddington to Bristol (Temple Meads) line, after being ousted by the first deliveries of the HST in the mid to late 1970s. A shortage of HST sets saw two daily diagrams returned to locomotive haulage - usually covered (one each) by Class 47 and Class 50 locomotives. The 09.10 and 15.18 from Bristol, along with the 12.20 and 17.20 from Paddington, tended to be Class 50 hauled with an air-conditioned set of Mk 2 coaches. A similar diagram but based at Old Oak Common utilised a set of Mk 3 coaches with a generator van included for electric train heating (ETH), enabling more of the locomotive's power to be used for traction.

All these services remained timed at 125mph and drivers were given official encouragement to push

On 14 August 1980, 50050 *Fearless* roars through Wimbledon with an Exeter service. *Stephen Parker*

their locomotives hard in order to minimise time loss. This led to some high quality running and reports of Class 50s being driven at speeds well in excess of their permitted maximum of 100mph were commonplace. On 15 July 50050 took charge of the 12.20 Paddington - Bristol with nine coaches in tow. A detailed log of the run was published in an article written by Alex Bayliss for the *Class 50 News* - the journal of modern day Class 50 owners, the Class 50 Alliance. On this occasion, high but not overly excessive speed was utilised to cover the 71 miles from Reading to Bath in 47.37 minutes - at an average speed of 89.3 mph. 30 years on, the fastest journey time available between these stations is a comparatively lethargic looking

Opposite: Long before becoming a firm favourite for railtours, 50050 *Fearless* was selected to haul the 'West Riding Ltd' railtour from London Bridge to York on 10 March 1979 - it's first time on such a working. The typically grubby Class 50 attracts a lot of attention from enthusiasts at Bury St Edmunds. *Paul Winter*

55 minutes - albeit inclusive of two station stops.

In mid August, 50050 began a short residence on the Waterloo line, staying on the route for between one and two weeks. By the end of month it was back on more usual workings, relieving 50025 *Invincible* on the down sleepers from Paddington at Plymouth, before working the corresponding up train on the same night - 30 August. The Penzance sleeper services were known as the 'Up and Down Midnight' by Class 50 followers. On Saturday 4 October, more Bristol line HST replacement duties occupied 50050 before it headed down to Plymouth the next day on the 11.25 from Paddington. Monday saw the locomotive begin a new week with another visit to Waterloo.

The early months of 1981 again saw little change for 50050 as it continued to ply its trade primarily on the WR. These duties included the occasional run through to the Cotswolds from Paddington. On February 7 the locomotive suffered a bizarre failure at

Paddington - a stuck horn! A witness likened the resulting noise to "some aquatic creature in its death throes". By way of a change, 50050 made another appearance on the Bristol line HST replacement diagram in February when it took charge of the 11.10 from Temple Meads to Paddington. The same feature in *Class 50 News* revealed the non-stop run from Bath to Reading required less than 48½ minutes (average speed 87.7mph), even allowing for a fairly leisurely arrival after the driver shut off power well before Tilehurst and cruised in.

In the days when the HST's sheer pace was utilised to the full in railway timetabling, the booked schedule between Reading and Bath was around 41 minutes (103.8mph). This time was inclusive of three minutes engineering allowance however, lifting the net schedule to a hurricane like 111.9mph average speed.

One month later and it was a totally different story as 50050 began a long period out of service

A wonderfully symmetrical study of unrefurbished 50030 *Repulse* and 50050 between duties at Bristol on 17 February 1980.

John Chalcroft / www.railphotoprints.co.uk

at Laira depot. Initially stopped following a main generator failure, the decision was taken to exchange it for a replacement sent from Doncaster. This was carried out by the end of May but frustratingly further problems developed. It would be mid September before 50050 poked its nose out of the depot confines again, when it piloted an up train from Plymouth to Exeter. This method was often used by Laira for testing repaired locomotives, with the 1M85 07.40 Penzance - Liverpool the usually chosen train. After returning to Laira, 50050 was soon back in service taking the return working of an Eastbourne to Newquay charter for the Co-operative Society back as far as Westbury on 19 September. The outward leg had run a week earlier.

Late 1981 marked the final months of service for the Class 55 'Deltics', and mass coverage dominated the pages of the newly-launched *Rail Enthusiast* magazine. Unashamedly aimed at the young train spotter or locomotive 'basher', the new magazine's style immediately set it aside of the existing, occasionally stuffy established titles. The demise of such an iconic and

popular class of locomotive undoubtedly gave the new magazine a spectacular launch pad.

The final 'Deltic' hauled trains (for a while!) ran on the second day of 1982, after which time some of their fans looked for new classes to follow. Many opted to join the Class 40 bashers in the North West, but the days of these English Electric veterans were also numbered, and a growing number of younger locomotive fans began to tune into the Class 50s.

The Class 50 refurbishment programme created a mixture of unmodified and modified '50s', with an increasing number of locomotives appearing in the striking new 'large logo' livery. The fleet still retained many top link duties, and backed by plenty of positive photographic coverage in magazines such as *Modern Railways Pictorial* - popularity of the '50s' soared. All carried names, and from the spring of 1982 the Falklands Conflict led to regular appearances of names like *Conqueror* (50009), *Invincible* and, of course *Fearless,* in British daily newspapers and on the television. Encouraged by the new adulation for Class 50s, a supporters' club, the Class 50 Locomotive Group

(C50LG) launched in 1981, saw a huge increase in membership, to 722 by the end of 1982. The group's bi-monthly magazine *The Hoover* - a remarkably high quality amateur production for its time, kept fans up to date with all the news and workings until its demise through bankruptcy in 1983.

Late March began an eventful few days for 50050 beginning on the 28th when it failed at Camborne on the 'Up Midnight' after suffering an exhaust fire. Assistance was provided from Penzance by 50022 *Anson*, which pushed the train as far as Truro where it shunted the recalcitrant Class 50 to the sidings. A Class 37 was provided the following day to haul 50050 to Laira depot for repairs. Not long after, the '50' returned to traffic and was noted working a down freight through Devon on the afternoon of 31 March.

On Saturday 3 April, 50050 worked a charter train for the LNER Society to Plymouth and Dartmouth via Worting Junction. Four days later on 7 April, 50039 *Implacable* and 50050 double-headed the 07.26 Paignton - Paddington.

British Rail offered enthusiasts the chance of a closer look at Class 50s - and other locomotives too, when Laira depot held its first open day for ten years on 25 April. The C50LG seized the opportunity by adorning 50023 *Howe* at the depot with a headboard displaying the group's name. The same headboard also appeared at Plymouth station later in the day affixed to 50040 *Leviathan.* Meanwhile, 50050 kept out of the way at St Blazey depot.

The May 1982 timetable saw a drastic reduction of locomotive hauled trains on the Cotswolds Line, with the Paddington to Worcester services being curtailed at Oxford where passengers were invited to change for a DMU forward. Through workings to and from Hereford, two up in the morning and two down in the evening remained hauled and booked for a Class 50.

Appearances by 50050 on the Waterloo route in 1982 were few and far between, due to the unrefurbished locomotives being kept away where possible because of their poorer reliability. On 1 July, 50050 worked the 09.38 from Exeter and 17.00 from Waterloo, a diagram completed at Laira depot. This turn was booked to start at Eastleigh depot following servicing of the coaches, so it is likely that 50050 worked on the route the previous day. Services this summer were regularly subjected to short term alterations however, due to industrial action.

BR and its customers suffered massive disruption in the summer of 1982 as members of the train drivers' union ASLEF (Associated Society of Locomotive Engineers and Footplatemen) withdrew their labour in opposition to the proposed introduction of 'flexible rostering'. Most of the shutdowns were mercifully short, but July was marked by a continuous two week stoppage. During this time, 50050 resided at its home depot patiently awaiting work.

Back in action, *Fearless* busied itself on various top-link duties across the Western Region including trips up to Birmingham from both Plymouth and Paddington. The first week of August saw plenty of action culminating with a final hurrah on the Paddington to St Austell motor-rail services. These trains conveyed cars on bogie flat wagons, while the vehicles' owners and their families travelled to Cornwall by HST. In previous years, cars and passengers were conveyed on the same train with the car carriers marshalled behind the passenger coaches. The service was withdrawn at the end of the 1983 season.

On Sunday 8 August, 50050 worked west in a more conventional fashion when it powered the 1B22 09.25 Paddington - Plymouth. This service was a booked double-header on the 1A27 14.40 return and Laira depot provided 50027 as the pilot engine for an unrefurbished duo back to London.

Late August saw 50050 stopped for a fuel lift pump repair at Laira and then in late September it could find nothing more taxing to do than shuttling coaches between Old Oak Common and Paddington. These localised restricted duties were usually handed to locomotives returning to work following repairs. At the end of that month the 1A31 16.25 Oxford - Paddington produced train engine 50001 *Dreadnought* with 50050 joining it on test before being let loose on full duties again. This is likely to have been the final time the first two built Class 50s double-headed in original livery.

In the latter months of 1982, 50050 continued to give good service on Paddington workings supplemented by occasional cross-country jaunts between the West Midlands and Devon. There were more double-headers too as 50029 *Renown* joined *Fearless* at the head of the 07.40 Taunton - Paddington on 25 October. In early November, 50050 combined with 50009 to work the 'Up Midnight' from Penzance, a feat repeated in early December with an ex-works 50034 *Furious*.

Later that month however, 50050 disappeared from the radar before eventually being tracked down to Old Oak Common depot. The whole fleet of Class 50 locomotives had recently been slowed down to a new maximum permitted speed of 95 mph. BR explained this decision as being due to short, but heavily loaded newspaper trains affecting braking capability at higher speeds - the removal of the dynamic braking system during refurbishment had an additional negative effect here.

There were other, unofficial theories but whatever the reason for it, the restriction only lasted for 12 months - with no discernable changes to newspaper traffic being made in the period.

50050 departs from Birmingham New Street on 15 April 1982. *Pete Key*

The practice of recording the time taken by trains between stations, and speeds attained is long established and harks back to the days of infrequent, heavily loaded trains that often provided a stern test for the hauling locomotive. In the modern age as line speeds improved, significant reductions in journey times were possible using faster, more powerful diesel locomotives such as Classes 47, 50, 55, and the Inter-City 125 (HST). This encouraged analysis by enthusiasts and professionals alike of individual locomotive performances, sparking debate and argument, which often continues decades later.

In recent years, with additional station stops prevailing over minimum end to end journey times, the spotlight on train performance has shifted towards the quality or robustness of the timetable 'plan' rather than the exploits of the train or its crew. Early running is tolerated less than it was, while a late running train is more likely to be further delayed by other trains being given priority - than be given a clear run to make up time.

Through the 1980s, traditional diesel locomotive hauled trains remained common, and there were still many routes where an on-form locomotive, a clear road and a keen driver could make the difference between a standard run and a memorable one. Three examples of 'on the road' performance by 50050 are included in this book, starting with a journey from Oxford to Paddington on a Saturday afternoon in January 1989.

In the 1980s the vast majority of Paddington to Oxford services stopped at just one station en-route - Reading, leaving two sections of relatively high speed running before and after the call. Today, most similar services are formed of DMU stock and also call at Slough. They are typically timed a little slower than the locomotive-hauled trains they replaced nearly two decades ago.

Back in January 1989, following a morning bathed in glorious sunshine 50050 brought the stock for the 1F55 13.00 to Paddington into Oxford station under dark skies as the heavens opened. Passenger demand did not justify nine coaches on a Saturday afternoon and in truth outside peak times, similar trains often ran barely half full. The wet conditions may have contributed to the slightly hesitant start, but the train was going well when eased off just after Culham for the speed restriction at Didcot North Junction.

The schedule shown as far as Reading is current, and applicable to a Class 165/166 'Turbo' DMU. After deduction of engineering and pathing allowances, the net schedule to Didcot North Junction is eight and half minutes. Thus 50050 was 20 seconds shy of the

New Order at this point.

Normal practice on up runs was for the driver to coast on the Didcot avoiding line under green signals, until the route indicator came into sight for East Junction. Ironically if the train was being put on the relief line, the driver would open up straight away, whereas an indication for the main line meant full power had to be held back until the train had snaked across the junction 'ladder'.

Having finally accessed the main line, 1F55 continued in typical style with miles per hour (mph) rising into the mid 90s - but no more before the driver backed off in plenty of time for any adverse signals approaching Reading. Platform changes at Reading were commonplace as the signallers endeavoured to direct the faster locomotive hauled trains and HSTs to Platform Five, leaving Platforms Eight and Nine for the slower trains. Today 50050 coasted through Tilehurst straight to Platform Five. In spite of this restrained approach, the locomotive hauled train had cut one minute from the DMU schedule since Didcot North Junction.

The re-start from Reading was copybook and 50050 passed

Twyford in typical style. The schedule quoted is for a Class 47 and nine coaches (Summer 2001) - given a vigorous start from Reading, some Class 50s threatened to beat five minutes to Twyford, even with nine on. After reaching maximum service speed just after Maidenhead, *Fearless* had plenty of time in hand when passing Slough as it cruised effortlessly up the Thames Valley. Before Hayes & Harlington, the driver eased right down causing speed to fall - possibly a little too rapidly. To minimise the risk of holding up anything behind, a quick burst of power saw speed back up to 94mph at Hanwell, before the locomotive was eased again. This ensured observance of the 85mph maximum permitted speed for locomotive hauled trains at Acton Main Line.

With London in sight and an early arrival a formality, a restrained approach to Platform Eight concluded another uneventful journey from Oxford. Most locomotive hauled journeys required just over six minutes from West Ealing to the buffers, but in spite of taking an extra minute today - (Platform Eight is a long way from the main lines!), 50050 brought 1F55 to a stand well ahead of time.

First of the last

50050 *Fearless* arrives at Oxford hauling the empty stock in preparation for it working 1F55 to London Paddington on Saturday 21 January 1989.

Ian Horner

Performance Tables

Stations, locations in between, and their mileages are shown in the first two columns. At each station call, the mileage and the stop-watch are reset. The third column gives the schedule between stops (half minutes are indicated by H) and any allowances applicable - sometimes known as recovery time. The allowances are in effect, extra time in the schedule to compensate for:-

Engineering work - possibly a temporary speed restriction (TSR), additional time is shown in square brackets or a box. For example [2] would indicate two minutes allowance.

Performance - introduced in the 1990s, this is for general time loss and could include traction and rolling stock delays. This allowance would appear in diamond form, for example <2>.

Pathing - this is added time in a schedule where the train has to be held back because there is another train due just ahead of it. Shown in brackets (2), this allowance is common approaching junctions or stations.

The schedules advertised in the public timetable can differ to those worked to by railway operating departments. These differing schedules are often referred to as 'working book' and 'public book'.

The final two columns in each table show the time taken in minutes and seconds, with recorded train speeds along with any additional relevant information.

Saturday 21 January 1989   1F55 13.00 Oxford - Paddington

50050 + 8 x Mk2, 1 x Mk1 Coaches - 291/300 tons

Miles	Location	Sched & Allows	Time	Comments / mph
0.0	Oxford	0	00.00	...
5.1	Radley	[1]	05.34	...
7.3	Culham	(H)	07.11	84
9.6	Didcot North Jn	10	08.50	75*
15.0	Cholsey		13.06	UM - 87
18.7	Goring & Streatley		15.33	93
21.9	Pangbourne		17.35	94
24.8	Tilehurst		19.31	eased - 85
27.4	Reading	25	22.53	...
5.0	Twyford	5H	05.23	82
11.7	Maidenhead	10	09.47	99
15.0	Burnham		11.46	101
17.5	Slough	14	13.15	101
19.8	Langley		14.34	101
22.8	West Drayton		16.22	100
25.1	Hayes & Harlington	[2]	17.46	eased - 91
28.6	Hanwell		20.05	94
29.4	West Ealing		20.37	eased
31.7	Acton Main Line		22.12	82*
34.9	Westbourne Park		25.00	slow
35.9	Paddington	30	28.05	very slow approach to P8

* indicates a speed restriction

On 8 May 1983, *Fearless* stands inside Doncaster Works undergoing refurbishment, with three other '50s' in varying stages of refurbishment also visible.

Bob Foster

In December 1982, a dog tired 50043 *Eagle* entered the refurbishment programme, leaving just six unmodified Class 50s in traffic awaiting the call.

The impressive rate at which Doncaster Works had worked through the fleet meant that even though it had been overhauled only three years ago, 50050 found itself almost next in line for the treatment. In terms of shopping dates, 50049 *Defiance* was due next but had hardly worked at all since the summer thanks to a persistent low power problem.

The unmodified locomotives were not as reliable as the refurbished examples and an increasingly ropey 50050 had earned itself the nickname 'Teabag' from the Class 50 'bashers' - on account of all the leaks it suffered. The despatch of 50018 *Resolution* from Doncaster in mid-December led to both

50049 and 50050 being assigned northwards after the Christmas holidays. Transfer of 50050 was made via Severn Tunnel Junction yard and Toton depot in mid January, and it entered the works a few days behind 50049, to become the 46th Class 50 to join the refurbishment programme. This left a final unrefurbished quartet of 50002 *Superb*, 50014, 50027 and 50030 to slog on until May 1983 when 50014 headed north.

In early 1983 Doncaster Works held six Class 50s for refurbishment along with the Bristol collision damage victim 50044 *Exeter*. The total in Works briefly rose to eight after a fire-damaged 50027 arrived, and before 50007 *Hercules* departed.

Doncaster Works continued to release one refurbished Class 50 each month through spring and

into summer 1983. After 50049 left on 10 June, 50050 became due for release next. On Friday 1 July the locomotive was given a test run hauling the 1N21 08.44 Doncaster - Tyne Yard and back.

The following Thursday, 7 July 50050 made its way back to home turf by way of the 1V92 14.28 York - Plymouth, which reportedly started at Leeds due to industrial action although the service was normally routed via Pontefract. The immaculate locomotive was removed from the train at Gloucester after suffering from low power and was later worked up to London for display at Stratford depot open day on Saturday 9 July.

Fearless stayed in the London area after the event while a main generator fault was attended to, before reporting for more open day duties, at Brighton Lovers'

Walk depot the following weekend. Among the exhibits on the South coast were 1980s spotters' favourites; 33027 *Earl Mountbatten of Burma*, 47406 *Rail Riders* and 73101 *Brighton Evening Argus*.

On 50050's return to Laira, the replica ship's crests, removed at Old Oak Common for safekeeping in December, were refitted. The locomotive now wore the popular large logo livery - its first paint variation in 16 years of service. Other visible variations of a refurbished Class 50 included replacement of the bodyside window nearest the shutter blades (No.1 end) with an air intake grill, a small roof chimney above the main generator and the filling in of the roof recess at No.2 end. The headcode box was plated over (some Class 50s had received this modification pre-refurbishment, but not 50050) and the adhesion sandbox filling points were removed. A more obvious sign of a refurbished locomotive, especially at a distance was the fitting of a high intensity headlight on each cab end, centrally placed below the front windows.

Removal of the air filtration equipment altered the sound of the locomotives and the trait which earned them the 'Hoover' nickname was now gone. The name stuck with some, but other Class 50 followers began to refer to the locomotives as 'Vacs', acknowledging the origin of the name, while accepting that a change had been made! The 'Hoover' headboard, fashioned in the style of the vacuum cleaner manufacturer's logo had been adorning Class 50s - especially on railtours for some years, and would continue to do so. On 18 July, 50050 returned to normal service when it took charge of the 1S39 07.35 Plymouth - Glasgow, but failed at Gloucester after again suffering from low power.

News of Class 50s and reports of trains worked throughout summer 1983 can be sparse, due to this being the period between the demise of the Class 50 Locomotive Group and the emergence of the Class Fifty Society. The magazines of both these groups reported details of locomotive workings but summer 1983 fell into the gap and thus fewer notes are available. 20 years on however, the internet and a number of enterprising websites can bring rare and everyday workings to the attention of the dedicated web surfer. The *www.timewarp.abelgratis.com* site proclaims itself to be the "Largest collection of 1980's loco-hauled gen on the net!" and it is hard to argue against this when faced with pages of workings filed month by month every year from the mid 1970s through to the end of 1989.

A feature of this website is a section dedicated to Class 50 workings through Sheffield, which reveals that 50050 worked the 07.05 Plymouth - York and 14.28 return throughout on 13 October. This HST turn had returned to locomotive haulage due to cooling problems with new trains and provided a convenient means of getting Class 50s to and from Doncaster Works. Occasional out

and back trips were also made.

In December 1983, the refurbishment programme was completed with the release of 50014 from Doncaster Works. BR now, in theory, had a healthy fleet of 100mph capable locomotives set for years of reliable service. As it turned out, this coincided with another period of poor availability caused by a glut of main generator failures. During late 1983 and into early 1984, nine Class 50s had replacement main generators fitted at Doncaster Works or Laira depot. If this wasn't bad enough, accident damage sustained by 50022 at Acton Yard and 50041 *Bulwark* at Paddington just made matters worse. The pressure was on at Laira (LA) and Old Oak Common (OC) depots to keep as many locomotives in traffic as possible.

With the Class Fifty Society up and running in 1984, a new fan magazine was born and issue one of the *Class Fifty Forum* began reporting on the Class 50 scene. Early reports of 50050 in action included haulage of a morning Newbury to Paddington service with 50030 on 4 January. Three days later and with fleet availability at just 31 locomotives (62%) for 34 booked turns, *Fearless* powered

On its first working following release from Doncaster Works, 50050 was working back to the Western Region on 7 July 1983, and calls at Cheltenham Spa.   *John Grey Turner*

the 1A75 07.05 Hereford - Paddington. BR still managed to provide the promised Class 50 for special duties however, as 50004 took charge of the 1Z35 06.35 Plymouth – Victoria 'Grain Train' for F&W Railtours. Over on the Waterloo route, with two of six diagrams uncovered, the 'bashers' would have had to have chosen their moves with care.

On the first day of March 1984, 50050 headed for the Exeter to Waterloo line where it would spend most of the next two weeks working the former London & South Western Railway main line. At this time the route called for six locomotives per weekday with two each required at the start of every day at Laira, Eastleigh and London. The diagrams were not very productive and involved long periods of standing idle at both ends of the line. With 50050 starting at Laira with the empty stock for the 05.47 Exeter -

Waterloo and finishing at Eastleigh, this turn (230a) still covered around 600 Loaded Train Miles (LTM) however, higher than many in the rosters. Twelve days later on 13 March, *Fearless* completed its stint on the route with the 1V17 17.38 Waterloo - Plymouth and ensuing empty stock movement to Laira. By way of a change, the next duty taken was the 1M22 11.38 Plymouth - Manchester as far as Gloucester the following day.

In the early days of April, the sight of 50050 working the Waterloo to Exeter route became commonplace once again until Sunday 15 April, when it returned to Laira via the 20.10 from Waterloo. On the following Monday the locomotive worked up to Paddington at the head of the 3A27 06.15 empty newspaper vans from Plymouth, with 50042 *Triumph* for company. Following a

fortnight of duties on the Western however, the Southern came calling once again and 50050 returned for another brief stint in the land of the third rail. Right about this time, another availability problem manifested itself.

During a routine inspection at OC, cracks were found in the main frames of a Class 50 and this in time led to almost every member of the fleet having to undergo welding attention at Doncaster Works. The origins of the problem were never fully explained, but a commonly expressed theory was that poor track conditions on the eastern section of the Waterloo route were to blame. This ignored the fact that the first locomotives sent for frame welding repairs were all OC based, while the vast majority of duties on the southern were covered by LA locomotives.

Summer 1984 hailed the first new

First of the last

timetable period since the completion of the refurbishment programme, but the daily number of Class 50s required for service actually reduced to 31. At the same time, the new timetable promised some new and exciting workings for the fleet. Increased demand for rail travel saw the WR HST fleet at full stretch leading to one daily Paddington to Paignton working in each direction reverting to locomotive haulage. In addition, two new daily locomotive-hauled trains (each way) between Paddington and Penzance were entrusted to the class. Add to that the regular summer up and down daytime Penzance services, and there were now three morning departures from Paddington to the west booked for Class 50 haulage at; 09.40 (Penzance), 10.27 (Penzance) and 10.35 (Paignton). For later travellers there was also the 13.40 to Penzance.

On the first day of the new services, a sparkling 50003 *Temeraire* took the 1C32 10.35 'Torbay Express' from Paddington complete with a headboard, which was carried several times in May and early June. These workings attracted wide coverage in the railway press gaining the Class 50s further new admirers as they basked in more positive coverage.

Another development was a daily turn to Swansea, as the Class 50 off the 1M83 10.24 Penzance - Liverpool to Birmingham (for change to electric traction) would then work on into South Wales after relieving the 1V92 13.20 from Glasgow. In the first week of the revised timetable, 50050 worked this turn, continuing on to Paddington via the 1A03 01.50 from Fishguard Harbour, which changed locomotives at Swansea.

50050 *Fearless* waits to remove the stock of the 'Night Riviera' from Penzance on the morning of 24th June 1984. **Paul Bettany**

A few days later on the first summer Saturday of 1984, 50050 entered into the holiday spirit by taking the 1C35 11.15 Paddington - Paignton and 1A78 15.35 Paignton - Oxford. The locomotive continued in daily service but blotted its copybook at Paignton on 3 July when it failed with fire-bells ringing. This left the 1A48 11.05 Up 'Torbay Express' to Paddington without motive power until a replacement in the shape of 50035 was found.

50050 returned to traffic the next day and took the 2C74 16.35 Plymouth - Penzance and 1A02 21.35 Penzance - Paddington. Further action included taking a Malago Vale to Old Oak Common van train with 50040 'dead in train' on July 6 before replacing an HST the day after on the 20.15 Paddington - Plymouth. The latter working put the locomotive in perfect position to resume Waterloo line duties again the following day.

The summer saw fleet availability improve but the main frame crack repairs now being carried out in Works (the job being beyond the capabilities of LA or OC) continued to keep additional locomotives sidelined. In mid July, four Class 50s were undergoing or just arriving for intermediate overhauls at Doncaster with 50023 leaving following frame crack repairs. 50033 *Glorious* replaced it for frame crack attention, which would soon be incorporated into all intermediate overhauls. The ongoing accident damage repairs to the Paddington derailment victim 50041 would also keep Doncaster busy until early 1985.

On Sunday 22 July, 50050 and 50006 *Neptune* doubled up to power the 1A49 16.50 Plymouth - Paddington throughout but after arrival in London, *Fearless* went into hibernation at OC for the next month. The locomotive eventually re-emerged over the

August bank holiday weekend and continued to perform well while in traffic.

With the release of 50001 and 50013 *Agincourt* into service at the end of the summer following intermediate overhauls, the whole fleet had now been repainted into the large logo livery. The new paint scheme was never carried by all 50 locomotives simultaneously however, as 50007 had been transformed into a version of Great Western green livery and renamed *Sir Edward Elgar* in February. This was in connection with celebrations to mark 150 years of the Great Western Railway (and its predecessors), and plans were apparently being hatched to rename and repaint further Class 50s. There was however, much opposition to the name change, leading to vociferous protests, and no further makeovers were carried out. On the final day of the summer timetable Sunday 30 September, 50050 worked the 1O14 11.10 Paignton - Waterloo.

The winter diagrams saw the holiday trains removed for another year but the new daily London to Paignton and Penzance services remained in the rosters. An unusual winter working for 50050 occurred on Sunday 7 October when it hauled the diverted 07.57 Wolverhampton - Euston as far as Nuneaton, returning with the 08.00 from Euston back to Wolverhampton. Sunday diversions with electric locomotives being 'dragged' to Nuneaton and back entertained rail enthusiasts in the Midlands for years - although on this day the electric locomotive for the up train was not attached until Nuneaton.

On Friday 12 October, a fatal accident caused by a train passing a signal at danger near Wembley caused disruption on the WCML. In order to supplement the resulting reduced service into

50050 passes through Acton on 17 August 1983 with the 1627 Paddington - Didcot. The locomotive had only been back in traffic for just over one month following refurbishment. *Brian Morrison*

Euston station, some Paddington to Oxford services were extended to the West Midlands, thus employing 50050 on the 09.50 Paddington - Wolverhampton, 13.30 return and 18.50 back to Wolverhampton the following day. Still in the area on the following Sunday, 50050 again featured on the Nuneaton drags.

Class 50 activity in the Wolverhampton area was usually confined to the 1M61 17.40 Paddington - Wolverhampton and 1V10 06.22 Wolverhampton - Paddington, as performed by 50050 on 1 and 2 November. Both of these services were booked via High Wycombe. The next stage of the diagram saw haulage of the 1C32 10.35 Paddington - Paignton, followed by five short distance all stations local workings in Devon - complete with a rake of air-conditioned coaches.

At the end of November while hauling 1C32, 50050 failed at Westbury with loss of power and

required the assistance of a Class 47 onwards to Exeter. Both locomotives were removed at St David's in favour of 50016. This latest setback for 50050 again proved to be temporary as it returned to action two days later before continuing to provide good service to the end of the year. The final days of 1984 saw 50050 working several trains between Penzance and Paddington.

Once again there were numerous Class 50s laid up at Doncaster Works, with four shopped in December swelling the number greeting the arrival of 1985 in South Yorkshire to eight. Better news was the return to traffic of 50041 in January, 14 months on from its derailment at Paddington.

On Saturday 12 January, BR ran a day excursion from Redditch to Edinburgh, hauled by an electric locomotive. At this time the cross-city route had not yet been electrified so diesel traction was needed for the first leg from Redditch to Birmingham

New Street. Local Control provided 50050 to work the 5Z11 empty stock down to Redditch, which ran round to form the 1Z11 07.00 to Edinburgh back as far as New Street. To date, this is the one and only visit of a Class 50 to Redditch. The following day saw 50050 again helping out on the Nuneaton drags before returning to its home depot at the head of a cross country service.

For eight weekends starting on Saturday 19 January, Waterloo to Exeter services were diverted via Southampton due to engineering work taking place between Salisbury and Basingstoke. This wasn't a new diversion, but the revised train plan was published in the public timetable allowing more of the increasing band of Class 50 'bashers' to plan a few moves on what would be new track for many of them. The train plan remained as normal west of Salisbury with all the amendments being made on the eastern section. Typically the xx.10 departures from Waterloo were retimed to leave 32 minutes earlier at xx.38.

Keen to be involved in these revised workings, 50050 arrived at Laira late on Monday 28 January after hauling the 10.35 Paddington - Paignton, and subsequent Devon locals. The next day it headed up to Waterloo on the first service from Exeter and stayed on the line for the next few days. This spell of action culminated with haulage of the 06.38 and 18.38 down from Waterloo and the 12.20 up from Exeter on Saturday 2 February - all via Southampton. Two Saturdays later on 16 February a lively 50050 once again took the 10.35 'Down Torbay' from Paddington to Paignton.

On the Saturday after that however, 50050 was declared a failure at Paignton with the corresponding up service. The only locomotive available to take the train was a Class 47/3 (without train heating capability), but this was rectified at Exeter where 50035 took over.

After a few days out of traffic, 50050 emerged from Laira depot on the penultimate day of February and headed for Paddington on the 3A27 newspaper empties from Plymouth, this time double-headed with 50038 *Formidable*. The first two weeks of March saw the locomotive back in residence on the Waterloo route including another weekend on the Southampton diversions.

On Saturday 13 April, railtour duties provided a distraction from the norm as a Class 50 had been requested as traction for Hertfordshire Railtours' 'Dungeness Pebbledasher' trip around the south east corner of England. OC prepared 50050 for the duty, which started at Reading and toured a variety of routes in Kent including the branch lines to Grain, Folkestone Harbour and Dover Western Docks. Two Class

33s were provided to work the train down the line to Dungeness Power station. By the end of the day 50050 had passed 4,950 TOPS hours since refurbishment, thereby becoming due for an E-exam - the heaviest classified repair carried out at depot level. Given that 50050 had barely done 22 months service since leaving Doncaster in July 1983, this was a remarkable achievement and evident of the high standard of reliability delivered over the previous two years. In the same period, the locomotive covered an impressive 200,000 miles.

In early May, 50050 hauled the 1C09 06.35 Bristol - Plymouth, working in tamden with 37234. This often heavy train conveyed a mixture of passenger accommodation and mail vans, and produced a variety of double-headers attracting close attention from early rising local photographers and 'bashers'. With the May timetable changeover looming, 50050 resided at Laira depot undergoing maintenance in the form of a C-exam. At the same time, flashover damage was rectified as well as a blowing exhaust.

With the work complete in the first week of the new timetable,

the locomotive inevitably headed first for Waterloo. By the weekend it had migrated to the far west of England to join up with 50029 to haul the 1A50 09.32 Penzance - Paddington. This duty was shown in the new locomotive rosters as a booked double-header on the first and final two summer Saturdays of the season but only actually produced on the one occasion. On the final day of the month, 50050 hauled the 1C28 10.18 Paddington - Penzance but the driver was advised of a planned locomotive change at Exeter and that he should get a move on to minimise any delay while swapping over. Following an early arrival of some 20 minutes, the train continued westwards still to time with 50012 *Benbow* now in charge. 50050 reappeared later in the day on Devon local duties, making a quick pit-stop at Laira depot in the evening before relieving the overnight Manchester to Penzance train at Plymouth.

The good fleet availability of earlier in the year continued throughout the summer aided by a reduced number of locomotives stopped at Doncaster Works. At the start of June, there were only two Class 50s at Doncaster; 50045 *Achilles* and 50040 - both for intermediate overhauls. By

The 13.35 Exeter - Waterloo waits to start behind 50050 on 9 March 1985.
Ian Horner

50050 *Fearless* pauses at Exeter St Davids station on 22 November 1986 while working 1S71 07.30 Penzance - Aberdeen. ***Ian Horner***

mid month they had been joined by 50025 arriving for frame fracture repairs before 50033 replaced 50045 in the overhaul programme.

A spell of local work for 50050 in the west included an HST drag from Penzance to Plymouth on a service train with no rear power car. A regular coach was attached to the tail of the train in case assistance from the rear was required. On Saturday 6 July, 50050 worked the 1A48 11.45 Paignton - Paddington holiday train. The next day it was back in Devon hauling 50041 and 50049 to Laira depot for repairs. For a short time in August 1985, LA and OC depots managed to have 45 of the fleet in traffic, as availability touched 90%. New found confidence in the Class 50 was demonstrated over the bank holiday weekend as after being prepared at Laira, 50030 of Old Oak was entrusted to haul single handed a marathon overnight railtour from Plymouth to Edinburgh. Other than a discharge from the sludge tank while standing at a Northumbrian signal on canted track on the northbound run, the journey passed without incident. After dropping in at the Haymarket depot open day on Sunday 25 August, *Repulse* returned to

Plymouth overnight, with no reliability problems arising and without an assisting locomotive in sight!

Back on the Western, 50030 returned to its home depot by taking the 1A02 21.35 Penzance - Paddington 'Up Midnight' on Bank Holiday Monday 26 August. This duty was a booked double-header in Cornwall throughout the 1980s, with 50050 doing the pilot honours tonight. Four days later *Fearless* again featured on the train, this time working through to London with 50027 for company as far as Plymouth. 50050 continued to be kept busy throughout September before finally being stopped at the end of the month for the E-exam it became due for some five months earlier. Keeping good locomotives running even when overdue their E-exam was not unusual at the time. In mid October when 50050 returned to traffic, 50002/ 043/ 044/049 all remained in service overdue similar scheduled maintenance.

Back in action on Tuesday 15 October, 50050 firstly ran light diesel from Laira to Wellington to collect a Class 47, which had been dumped in the siding there after failing the previous day. The locomotive had suffered a shifted

tyre and special arrangements had to be made to get it to Bristol Bath Road depot. The next day saw 50050 back on normal duties as it took the 1C25 09.40 Paddington - Penzance as far as Plymouth, continuing west after relieving the 1V85 09.23 Newcastle - Penzance. The next few days work included the 6B54 freight turn in the West and a quick visit back to the LMR on the 1M82 20.00 Cardiff - Crewe and 1V01 02.04 return mail and passenger trips. This latter duty became another popular turn with Class 50 'bashers' in spite of the rather unsocial hours involved.

After another good year of service, 50050 closed out 1985 stopped at Laira for engine repairs, which were completed by the first weekend of 1986. Unfortunately the New Year did not start well as a main generator flashover occurred soon after re-entering service. Following inspection of the damage at Laira, it was decided to fit a replacement component at Doncaster Works, and take the opportunity to carry out frame fracture repairs at the same time. Transfer north was made via Severn Tunnel Junction Yard where 50050 was noted on 16 January. Four days later, a simultaneous entry was made to the works with 50005 *Collingwood*, which was due a classified overhaul. While at Doncaster it was decided to simply change 50050's whole power unit rather than split the engine from the main generator and so engine IH6942 was exchanged for IH6965 (recently ex-50008). The crucial under-frame crack repairs were

Opposite: With the village of Kingham visible in the background, 50050 *Fearless* passes Daylesford on 8 May 1986 with the 1B46 17.05 Paddington - Hereford service. Although an attractive livery when freshly applied, this view clearly shows why a light grey roof was not a good idea on a Class 50. ***Martin Loader***

also carried out and all work was completed by the end of February. In early March, 50050 returned home on the 1V95 15.38 Leeds - Plymouth van train, and was soon back at work on normal duties in Cornwall.

With its new engine and generator set in place, 50050 would become one of the most dependable Class 50s over the next 16 months - up to its final overhaul. Duties through the rest of March continued to be varied, including another Birmingham to Paddington run arising after disruption on the WCML. On the 26th the locomotive worked a special train including the high speed track testing coach northwards through Devon, before encountering an unusual incident two days later.

On Friday 28 March while heading the 1C11 06.50 Swindon - Penzance, a collision with an unlucky swan near Uphill Junction resulted in a shattered windscreen. The damage was repaired over the weekend at Bristol Bath Road depot and 50050 worked down to its home depot on Monday morning with 50007 on the 1C09 06.35 Bristol - Plymouth. Coolant loss resulted in a more normal failure at Birmingham New Street the following Saturday after arrival on 1S71 from Penzance. Repairs were made at Saltley and the locomotive quickly headed south on the Glasgow sleeper train to Bristol, where an A-exam was carried out at Bath Road depot.

The summer 1986 locomotive diagrams raised the weekday requirement for Class 50s up to 36 with the new rosters showing significant alterations to the West of England services. The 09.40 and 13.40 trains from Paddington were withdrawn and replaced by a single locomotive-hauled departure at 11.45. Similarly in the Up direction, the 09.32 and 16.17 from Penzance were replaced with one train departing at 10.00. The Penzance trains, once known by some as 'Jumbos' due to their length (13 coaches, sometimes more) had proved unpopular with passengers due to their slow schedules - many had simply opted to catch the next HST. The Down 'Torbay Express' now left at 11.10, just in front of another Class 50 turn, the 11.17 to Oxford as the hourly Thames Valley services were reworked to leave at xx.17.

The summer Saturday holiday trains reappeared of course and there was a change on Friday nights as the relief to the 'Down Midnight' was redirected to Newquay instead of Penzance. This formation (a Mk 1 commuter set usually) would then work back to London as the 1A60 11.35 Newquay - Paddington on Saturday morning. On the first weekend of the new timetable, 50050 covered this diagram

The life & times of 50050 *Fearless*

although being so early in the season, patronage was not great.

In June 1986, a major marketing campaign heralded British Rail's re-launching of its London and South East sector as Network SouthEast (NSE). A huge exercise in re-branding, the likes of which hadn't been seen on BR since the switch to corporate blue livery, this was the prelude to a massive makeover for stations and rolling stock right across the South East. A new livery was conceived - a striking red, white and light blue design complete with branding in huge lettering along the flanks of NSE locomotives. This was especially noticeable when seen next to traditional BR blue and grey livery.

A press event held to launch Network SouthEast at Waterloo station featured a freshly reliveried Class 50, OC's 50023 with a short rake of similarly treated Mk 2 coaches. Having been parked outside the station shielded from view by an old EMU set, 50023 was driven into Waterloo to face the cameras with a repainted Class 455 EMU.

50017 of LA had been prepared in the new livery too, and appeared at Paddington in the evening peak period to take out an Oxford train. In order to attract more people on to the new railway in the south east, NSE held the first of many 'Network Days' on Saturday 21 June. For the princely sum of £3, unlimited access to the whole NSE network could have been yours.

The summer proved a good one for Class 50 fleet availability with the 36 locomotives required for daily service being regularly beaten through June and July. Sightings at Doncaster Works continued to decline with only 50035 and 50037 Illustrious noted in July, both undergoing intermediate overhauls. Three additional visits for unclassified repairs (including 50035 for rectification work) were made from August into September but the front line held firm with plenty of locomotives available for work.

From late summer 1986, the responsibility for carrying out classified overhauls was split between Laira depot and Doncaster Works ahead of the Devonshire depot taking full responsibility from April 1987. Additional lifting facilities were installed at Laira to aid power unit removal during the overhaul - now referred to as an F-exam, as part of the new Cost Effective Maintenance plan. Reconditioned major components such as engine, main generator and bogies would be sent down from Crewe Works for refitting during the exam, significantly reducing the time each locomotive spent out of service.

First of the last

The first Class 50 to be so treated, 50026 *Indomitable* arrived at Laira over the August Bank Holiday weekend and returned to service in the first week of October.

Availability and reliability may have improved but failures still occurred of course. On 6 June after performing well on its previous working, 50050 got no further than Basingstoke on the 1V19 19.10 Waterloo - Exeter. A Class 33 took the train onwards and the errant Class 50 was deemed fit enough to work the 2V54 06.09 Salisbury - Exeter the next morning, although it did not continue with the rest of the diagram.

In July, while most Class 50s behaved themselves, 50050 managed to fail four times. The first occurred on the 11th when it ran into trouble at Truro while working the 1C11 06.45 Swindon - Penzance. A Class 47 was summoned to haul the train over the last 26 miles to Penzance. On the 23rd while in charge of the 1S71 07.30 Penzance - Aberdeen, *Fearless* got no further than Bodmin Parkway before expiring in a cloud of smoke caused by fuel leaking on to the bogies. A Class 37, no doubt swiped from local clay train duties, gave the train a push to Plymouth where 50004 was on hand to continue in more usual fashion to London. The next two failures, first at Birmingham New Street, and then at Paignton suggested that repairs following the Bodmin incident had not been wholly successful. The delinquent 50050 was towed back to Laira by another Class 47 before taking a few days off while more repairs were carried out.

Opposite: 50050 basks in the morning sun at Penzance with the 08.55 to Newcastle on 6 September 1985.

Paul Winter

Reappearing in traffic on the first day of August, 50050 quickly got back in the groove and worked well through to being stopped for a D-exam in late October. An interesting double-header occurred on 1 September, when 50007 and 50050, possibly rehearsing for future railtour appearances together, worked the 1C11 06.45 Swindon - Penzance.

Later in the month, 50050 hauled the Birmingham Lawley Street to Nottingham and return freightliner services, an occasional job for a Class 50 between passenger turns in 1986. From the October timetable change, the 1S61 07.35 Cardiff - Glasgow was rostered for a pair of '50s' as far as Birmingham New Street on a Saturday morning. This was the result of a diagramming imbalance and after arrival in the Midlands both locos would run to Saltley for a few hours before splitting up and working trains to Paddington and back to South Wales in the evening.

The first weekend - Saturday 4 October - saw 50024 *Vanguard* join 50050 at the head of 1S61 with plenty of 'bashers' taken along for the thrash up the Lickey Incline and into Birmingham. Later in the day, 50024 worked to Paddington while 50050 returned to Cardiff after taking over the 1V90 14.20 from Glasgow at New Street station. The next day after a rest at Canton depot *Fearless* took the lightweight 1M37 16.45 Cardiff - Birmingham and 1V95 20.31 return service, before working the empty stock to Swindon on Monday morning, to form the 1C11 06.45 to Penzance. That day ended working the 'Up Midnight' in multiple with 50022.

Before being returned to traffic after its D-exam in the autumn, the yellow areas on 50050's driving cabs were given a new coat of paint. These had been looking a little shabby but the rest of the locomotive was deemed fine and left alone. Once again, the initial workings following heavy depot attention were very much confined to the west, including hauling a failed HST set into Penzance on 12 November. The locomotive also became a regular sight hauling the 1E91 09.33 Penzance - Newcastle as far as Plymouth.

A return to full service duties soon followed including haulage of the 1C39 11.45 Paddington - Penzance throughout on 18 November, before leading 50041 on the 'Up Midnight' as far as Exeter. 50050 then headed for a few days on the southern. The winter 1986/87 locomotive diagrams, maintained the daily Class 50 requirement at 36 for an assortment of duties including; express and local passenger work, van trains, freight trains in Devon and car traffic from Morris Cowley near Oxford. In addition to diagrammed work, HST replacements on the Paddington to Bristol route remained common.

Towards the end of 1986 rumours began circulating concerning the supposed imminent withdrawal from service of one Class 50. This was apparently due to the distribution of the national locomotive fleet among the new BR business sector managers only finding homes for 49 of the 50 Class 50s. If this were true then any locomotives becoming due for overhaul in the first months of 1987 would be at risk of becoming surplus to requirements. One railway publication of the time sufficiently disbelieved the situation to insist that one sector would be forced to take on the extra locomotive, but times were changing.

With a diminishing annual subsidy from central government, British Rail had to act on cost management and the still massive locomotive and rolling stock fleet cried out for reform. Ultimately

50050 *Fearless* accelerates away from Oxford and passes Hinksey Yard on 14 March 1987 with the 1F35 14:00 Oxford to Paddington. Network SouthEast's coach repainting programme was well ahead of locomotive repainting, so it was quite common at the time to see complete rakes of NSE Mk 1s hauled by Large Logo Class 50s.   ***Martin Loader***

this led to the condemnation of 50011 *Centurion* in February 1987. The locomotive was due an intermediate overhaul, but the deciding factor in it being chosen for the chop was that it hadn't received frame crack repairs at Doncaster Works. Instead of going straight to the scrapyard however, 50011 began a new life at Crewe Works acting as a static test bed for newly overhauled power units. On completion of testing, the power unit would then be sent by road to Laira depot for installation to Class 50s during the F-exam process.

At the turn of the year, another popular Class 50 story was that up to nine locomotives were about to be taken on by the newly created railfreight sector, possibly for hauling trains of spoil created by Channel Tunnel excavations. Some of the railway press went so far as to print a list of candidates by painted number, which included

50050. It was widely expected that the first Class 50 to enter Doncaster Works in 1987 would be converted for freight use, to become the trial locomotive ahead of further conversions later in the year. This put 50048 (not on the list of nine, but sent to Doncaster in January) squarely in the frame but when it emerged in the middle of March - its red, white and blue livery indicated it was headed for use by NSE, which indeed it was. After ten years of carrying out repairs on Class 50s, this was the last classified overhaul carried out by Doncaster Works - from now on Laira depot was on its own.

Bitterly cold weather blown in from Siberia took up residence over the United Kingdom in January 1987, resulting in a long period of travel difficulties and disruption affecting all modes of transport. Stories of trains arriving at their destinations several hours late were commonplace and

there were many cancellations. Locomotive availability plummeted but 50050 managed to keep busy most days - the risk of failure from freezing clearly reduced through being kept running!

There were many instances of double-heading throughout the month with; 50034, 50027 and 50035 all partnered on the 'Up Midnight' through to Exeter. On 19 January, 50018 fresh from its F-exam at Laira was tested on the 2C66 07.27 Plymouth - Penzance with 50050 taken along for insurance. Both locomotives headed straight home by taking the 1M83 10.30 Penzance - Liverpool as far as Plymouth.

Friday 13 February was an unlucky day for 50011 as it was towed from OC to LA, never to haul a passenger train again. Haulage was provided by 50050 with 50049 being picked up en-route at Exeter. In preparation for its withdrawal from frontline service, 50011's nameplates were removed and its bogies exchanged for those supporting 50041, which were in worse condition.

On 6 March, an unusually long train was created at Salisbury when two vehicles from the Venice Simplon Orient Express (VSOE) train were added to the 1O15 05.48 Exeter - Waterloo, hauled by 50050. This proved a convenient method to get the extra coaches to Stewart's Lane depot, but must have caused concerns through excessive length at Waterloo station. By the end of the month, *Fearless* had clocked up 7,500 TOPS hours and was edging closer to classified overhaul (F-exam) time again. With 50007 and 50046 *Ajax* now stopped for their own F-exams, the Class 50s running the highest hours were; 50029 and 50028 *Tiger* - with 50027 and 50050 running neck and neck behind. With 12 F-exams planned for the 1987/8 financial year, these four plus eight other locomotives would be treated and so become the likely final locomotives left in traffic four years hence.

The May 1987 timetable and associated locomotive rosters brought about the biggest shake up of Class 50 duties for some time. The weekday requirement remained for 36 locomotives but the new 'sectorised' workings saw Class 50s virtually eliminated from Paddington to the West of England services as well as the Hereford trains and cross-country duties to the Midlands. The future for the class did not look good as Inter-City confirmed its intention to do without, and with new generation DMUs expected to replace locomotive-hauled trains in Devon and Cornwall soon, more withdrawals would surely be inevitable.

Small consolation was that for now, Class 50s - and their NSE sector coaches were still required

for weekend holidaymaker trains to the West of England. Such trains were in decline now due mainly to the UK consumer losing patience with the unpredictable British weather and the rise of cheap package holidays in the Mediterranean - sunshine guaranteed. For a few years yet however, a healthy procession of additional trains would head for Devon and Cornwall at weekends.

Still allocated to Laira depot but also to the Parcels Sector locomotive pool (code RXXA), 50050 worked the Waterloo line as the new timetable commenced on Monday 11 May. Two days later it appeared at Weymouth at the head of the 16.18 from Bristol, returning to Temple Meads at 19.35. At the weekend 50050 substituted for unavailable Class 47s on cross-country Inter-City trains including the overnight Edinburgh/Glasgow to Plymouth service on Sunday night.

After three more days on similar duties, Thursday saw 50050 allocated to turn No.225 - a new diagram that started out on local passenger duties in Devon before

heading up to Bristol in the afternoon. An early evening out and back run to Taunton followed before the day was concluded heading the 1C80 22.35 Bristol - Exeter. This turn became popular with Western Class 50 'bashers' and was a convenient way of keeping a locomotive in traffic, when restricted to local work by Laira. At this time, the allocation of locomotives to turns and specific pools was largely nothing more than a paper exercise. A Class 50 was still a Class 50 and for now at least, the operating authorities continued to treat them all as one single fleet.

With the railfreight project confirmed as on, a locomotive still needed to be nominated for conversion for freight use during its upcoming F-exam. Prime candidates included 50043/049/050 - all of which were due for overhaul this summer, although both 50049 and 50050 were running power units well short of shopping hours. There was an apparent reluctance at Laira, and possibly beyond to see the doyen of the class, 50050 selected for the role, but with Railfreight

In a typical 1980's scene, 50050 stands at Plymouth awaiting departure on the 11.00 Plymouth - Penzance. *Peter Goodman*

planning to run trials in the autumn, the chosen locomotive would have to be stopped soon for the conversion work to take place.

In late June, just as 50029 returned to service following its F-exam, 50050 was placed on a local restriction and limited to 70mph (on TOPS only). This kept it handily placed in the West for taking to Laira depot once 50029 was ready for a full return to traffic. After working turn 225 again on Monday 29 June, 50050 worked the 1E06 14.15 Plymouth - Leeds vans to Gloucester the following day before returning to Plymouth in time for breakfast on the first day of July. In the afternoon *Fearless* hauled the 2C76 16.58 Plymouth - Penzance before returning to Laira.

On 2 July and by now in need of a bogie change due to worn tyres, Laira stopped 50050 for its fifth and what would prove to be its final classified overhaul. Exactly four years on since being released from Doncaster Works following refurbishment, the locomotive had run up 8,251 TOPS hours, indicating that shopping was due once again. With its two main components being barely 16 months old however, the locomotive could easily have been pushed on for longer - for want of a bogie change. Being stopped now however, ensured that 50050 would remain a 100mph Class 50/0 locomotive with NSE when it returned to traffic.

The railfreight project locomotive would be the next one stopped for an F-exam. Arriving at Laira in early August, 50049 retained its 'half life' power unit, which was de-rated to 2,400 bhp and received a new pair of bogies re-geared to give better starting performance under heavy load. To distinguish these modifications from a standard Class 50, the locomotive was renumbered 50149 and painted into railfreight triple grey livery with vivid red and yellow 'general' markings applied on each body side. The project ultimately failed because of the removal of the rail-sanding equipment during refurbishment. The unique Class 50/1 remained in service for around 18 months, being used primarily as cover in Cornwall while collision damage sustained by two Class 37s was repaired at Crewe Works.

Analysis of the fleet in the first week of July revealed the star performers, with the highest productivity in the first six months of 1987. Top accolade went to 50009 with almost 1,500 hours accumulated, and 50027 not far behind on 1,400. Next up were 50034/040/044/049/050, all in the 1,300 - 1,400 hours bracket, a fine effort by all in such a relatively short period of time. Of these

seven machines, only *Furious* and *Exeter* had been recently overhauled and five were based at Laira.

The Devonshire depot had its work cut out at this time. In addition to the F-exam now started on 50050, Laira completed a D-exam for 50027 and a protracted E-exam for 50020. Remarkably the F-exam for 50028, started in mid June continued through to early September meaning *Tiger* was effectively overtaken by *Fearless* during the work. Doncaster Works was no longer available for help with overhauls and major unclassified work, and the transfer of a severely failed 50047 *Swiftsure* down from Old Oak Common just added to the workload.

With spare parts at a premium, the decision was taken to withdraw another Class 50 - this

The sad distinction of being the first Class 50 to be withdrawn fell to 50011 *Centurion*, which was stood down in February 1987. In happier times it is seen at Plymouth in August 1983.   *Ian Dobson*

being 50006, which had lain idle since suffering a main generator flashover in early June. *Neptune* donated parts from its supremely reliable engine however, enabling 50020 to re-enter traffic. The

donor locomotive was axed as it was almost due for an overhaul and just like 50011 previously, it had not had any frame fracture repairs carried out - two down, 48 more to go.

Above: 50050 stands at Salisbury on 17 April 1987, before NSE red became the norm at stations across Network SouthEast territory. Just over three months later and 50050 would emerge in NSE livery.

Tim Rogers

Opposite: 50050 works the 08.11 Exeter - Waterloo on 8 May 1987, passing through Basingstoke.

Bob Foster

As described in Chapter Five 50050 took charge of the last train of the day from Exeter to Waterloo in mid August 1987. Good running west of Salisbury was demonstrated by the gain of over one minute on the 11 minutes allowed between Gillingham and Tisbury. Further gains to Salisbury (in spite of a 40mph TSR) boded well for the eastern section of the route too, but a rare signal stop just before the tunnel interrupted the start from Salisbury station. In spite of this setback, 50050 flew up Porton Bank, and had its train up to 94mph at Grateley before touching 98mph before Andover - where the arrival was still two minutes earlier than scheduled!

Following local station stops at Whitchurch and Overton (not shown in the table), *Fearless* got back into its stride, and the high speeds between stations on the Basingstoke to Woking section speak for themselves. To reel off the nine miles from Hook to Farnborough at over 100mph was just stunning, and this standard was maintained across the entire 14 miles to Brookwood.

A clear run into Woking might have yielded a time in the region of 16¾ minutes (84mph), but this was not to be. The final leg of 50050's journey to Waterloo should have taken no more than 23 minutes. Thanks to a 20mph TSR at Weybridge and a signal stop near Vauxhall however, more than half an hour was actually required - such was the frustration of the Exeter to Waterloo line!

The second run describes a double-header on the 08.11 from Exeter in September 1989. Following a few days out of service at Laira, 50050 returned to traffic on the morning Newton Abbot to Exeter train, paired with 50018. The duo remained coupled together, and then took the next Waterloo service.

With a full formation of Mk 2 coaches in tow, the pair was over one minute quicker from Sherborne to Templecombe than the usual eight minutes required by a single locomotive. A signal check approaching Gillingham disappointingly deprived the pair of achieving even time (one mile

per minute) or better - arrivals in less than seven minutes from Templecombe were common, even with a single engine.

The climb to Semley presented no problems whatsoever and 50050/ 018 were being reigned in long before passing the closed station at the summit - a full 40 seconds faster than a good run with a single Class 50. By free-wheeling back down the grade to Tisbury, the driver used about half a minute more than he could have done, but there was no need for showboating and the train remained on time. Over exuberant driving resulting in station overruns was common on the Exeter to Salisbury section, with Axminster and Sherborne in particular featuring regularly in despatches!

Re-starting from Salisbury, full power was quickly applied for the sprint up Porton Bank and on to Grateley, but the locomotives were eased well before the station after breaking into the early 90s mph. Speeds of over 100mph were common down to Andover, but today the driver held steady at around 90mph yet still managed to beat the schedule by over four minutes. On the racing ground east of Basingstoke, high speeds came easy before the pair was eased right off before Farnborough - passed at 85mph. Just to show what was in the locker if required, a brief surge up to 100mph at Brookwood preceded the usual signal check approaching Woking.

Arrivals at Woking in less than 17½ minutes from Basingstoke (80.4mph) were common but unpredictable due to regulation issues approaching the junction with the Guildford lines. A fast run with a smart arrival at Woking would take just over three minutes from Brookwood, so there was still potential for a sub 17 minutes (82.8mph) time today given the right circumstances. The schedule for contemporary DMU traction between Basingstoke and Woking is currently 18 minutes.

50050 and 50018 arrive at Whimple on 29 September 1989.
Peter Horner

First of the last

ove: 50050 leads 50018 *Resolution* away from Woking on last section of the 08.11 service from Exeter to Waterloo 29 September 1989.　　　　　**Ian Horner**

Miles	Location	Schedule & Allowances	Thursday 13 August 1987 1024 19.47 Exeter - Waterloo 50050 + 8 x Mk2 Coaches - 258/265 tons		Friday 29 September 1989 1048 08.11 Exeter - Waterloo 50050/50018 + 9 x Mk2 Coaches - 290/300-310 tons	
			Time	Comments / mph	Time	Comments / mph
0.0	Sherborne	0			00.00	...
3.7	Millborne Port				04.15	79
6.1	Templecombe	8			06.50	...
6.8	Gillingham	8	00.00	...	07.33	sigs/-
4.1	Semley		n/r	...	04.31	...
8.0	Tisbury	11	09.44	...	09.18	...
12.6	Salisbury	15H	13.49	TSR 40*/-	12.55	...
	Signal stop		01.54 / 02.10	0 mph		
1.1	Salisbury Tunnel Jn	3	03.30	est passing time	01.57	...
5.4	Porton		n/r	...	05.29	81
11.0	Grateley		11.52	94/98	09.23	eased - 91
17.4	Andover	18H	16.19	...	14.23	...
18.5	Basingstoke	18H	00.00	...	16.58	sigs Worting Jn
5.6	Hook		05.16	...	04.42	eased - 97
7.9	Winchfield		06.47	92	06.08	98
11.3	Fleet		08.44	*103*	08.11	97
14.6	Farnborough		10.38	*104*	10.18	eased off - 85
19.8	Brookwood		13.43	*101*	13.42	100
23.5	Woking	19H	18.45	sigs/-	18.22	sigs/-

See page 29 for explanation on performance tables.
Figures in *italics* denote average speed from previous timing point.

* indicates a speed restriction

The life & times of 50050 *Fearless*

The sea wall at Dawlish provided many opportunities for photographers and the rugged and scenic landscape in the area made for the some wonderful sights. 50050 heads 1V12 11.59 Portsmouth Harbour - Plymouth through Horse Cove at Dawlish on 7 July 1988. *Paul Robertson*

On 31 July 1987, 50050 emerged from Laira depot resplendent in the new revised NSE livery - the first Class 50 to be so treated. The new style was neater in appearance with the stripes running horizontally along the full length of the locomotive, not tapering up to the cab side windows as on the earlier versions. There was also a lot less white paint in evidence on the new variation.

As expected on release into service, 50050 was kept to local duties for a suitable shakedown period extending through early August. On the 13th however, Laira let go of the leash and 50050 worked the morning Totnes to Exeter local service, followed by the 08.11 up to Waterloo and 15.10 back down to Exeter. The day ended with a barnstorming run up to London on the 19.34 from Exeter, including covering Salisbury to Andover in less than 16½ minutes despite a brief signal stop before Salisbury tunnel. The driver then proved 50050's high speed credentials on the Basingstoke to Woking section, hammering through the 14 miles between Hook and Farnborough at an average speed of just over 100mph. The locomotive returned to Laira on Saturday night, enabling it to be used on the Sunday morning's 2C66 11.00 Plymouth - Penzance, for the third consecutive time.

Two days later on 18 August, 50050 returned to the Waterloo route starting with the 2C32 06.40 Totnes - Exeter again followed by two up and one down Waterloo runs. After ending the day in London it crossed over to the Western Region to spend Wednesday the 19th on Thames Valley duties. This preceded an overnight expedition to Penzance and a leisurely run back to Plymouth on the 1S15 12.10 Penzance - Glasgow Salkeld Street van train. Instead of returning to Penzance as diagrammed however, 50050 made a swift return to London heading a 15.12 relief train to Paddington. It was back to the Waterloo route on 21 August starting with the first down service from Waterloo. This few days of operation demonstrated how Class 50s could be swapped between Southern and Western duties quite easily.

The remainder of August saw the locomotive's services shared chiefly between the Waterloo line and Provincial Sector workings in the West of England. The month

First of the last

closed however, with 50050 working from Old Oak Common once again.

In early September, 50050 made a couple of appearances on the 17.53 Swindon - Longbridge and 22.41 return motor components trains. These workings regularly produced a Class 50 at the time as did similar duties from Morris Cowley, near Oxford. A few days later *Fearless* escaped back to Devon for a B-exam before starting another week on the Waterloo line from Monday 7 September.

From the middle of September, 50050 hid away at OC for a whole month while radiator repairs were carried out. The locomotive finally emerged on Thursday 20 October when it was given a test run as pilot engine to 50036 on the 1F12 08.20 Paddington - Oxford. All was not well however, and 50050 remained on the sidelines at the weekend, now with exhaust problems. By the following

Tuesday, 50050 had returned to its home depot for engine repairs after which it stayed local for a few days before being sent up to Waterloo again on 31 October.

At the end of a month spent almost exclusively on the Southern, 50050 ran into trouble at Grateley while working the 1V01 01.45 Waterloo - Yeovil Junction on 26 November. A main generator flashover had occurred, but the driver managed to coax the train along the favourable grade to Salisbury where a Class 33 was on hand to take over. The Class 50 remained in the formation and was shunted out at Salisbury on arrival of the 2O91 05.15 return working from Yeovil.

After being transferred to Laira for repairs, 50050 quickly returned to traffic and worked a train into Meldon Quarry on the final day of November. The next day the locomotive took the 3A27 06.55 Plymouth - Paddington and 3B07 15.50 Paddington - Bristol

van trains before venturing into Cornwall again at the head of the 1C11 06.45 Swindon - Penzance service on the day after that.

The irresistible attraction of the Waterloo line proved too much again as 50050 headed towards Southern metals on Thursday 3 December. Turn 218 started with the 2C99 05.00 Laira - Exeter, then the 1O12 06.42 Exeter - Waterloo, 1V13 13.10 Waterloo - Exeter and 1O22 17.33 Exeter - Waterloo. After taking fuel at Stewart's Lane depot, *Fearless* continued with turn 219 on Friday heading 1V01 01.45 Waterloo - Yeovil Junction, 2O91 05.15 Yeovil Junction - Salisbury, 2L10 06.40 Salisbury - Waterloo, 1P15 09.25 Waterloo - Portsmouth Harbour, 1V12 12.03 Portsmouth Harbour - Paignton, 2C47 16.40 Paignton - Exeter, and finally the 5V15 ECS from Exeter to Laira. Over the two days out from and back to Laira, these workings would have clocked up around 1,135 miles.

Positively sparkling following its repaint into the revised version of Network SouthEast livery, 50050 stands at Penzance on 1 August 1987. This was the first Class 50 to carry this variation of the colour scheme, which became the standard NSE livery scheme on all future repaints, although a darker shade of blue was adopted on later repaints.

Tim Rogers

The following day, 50050 worked the 3A27 06.55 Plymouth - Paddington empty newspaper vans before working back west overnight on the 1C06 23.25 Paddington - Penzance sleepers, running via Newbury, Hawkeridge Curve and Bristol Temple Meads. On the following Monday 50050 worked turn 225 again, concluding as booked with the 1C80 22.35 Bristol - Exeter. On Tuesday, the locomotive started the day working the 2C68 07.02 Exeter - Penzance, then 1S15 12.26 Penzance - Glasgow vans to Plymouth, 2C74 15.57 Plymouth - Penzance and 1F88 18.30 Penzance - Plymouth. This last two days would have yielded a less impressive 820 miles approximately, although well supplemented by a whole host of run-round moves! The early days of December demonstrated yet again the wide variety of duties still employing Class 50s.

Mid-December, saw a brief return to the Waterloo route before 50050 closed the year working from OC, mainly on Thames Valley services to and from Oxford. At least one trip was made to Birmingham on the 1M20 09.17 from Paddington and 1V69 13.11 return. After fuelling at OC on 27 December, 50050 worked down to Bristol for onward movement to Laira for planned maintenance. This transfer was completed by double-heading with 50002 on the 1C09 06.35 Bristol - Plymouth the following day, after which 50050 was then stopped for a C-exam which would be completed in the New Year.

With the expected withdrawal of 50014 being confirmed in mid December, the number of Class 50s remaining in traffic at the turn of 1988 stood at 47. By early March, the final classified overhauls (F-exams) would be complete, meaning the next overhaul due date for each locomotive effectively became its date for withdrawal from service.

There was still plenty of work for the class, but the large scale introduction of new generation DMUs on Provincial services planned from the May timetable, would soon reduce the daily demand for Class 50s.

After conclusion of its C-exam on New Year's Day 1988, 50050 returned to the fray on the 2nd, when it worked up to Exeter to take the 09.36 to Waterloo. Duties through January and February were primarily an unremarkable mixture of Waterloo and Thames Valley line trains with the occasional trip to Birmingham or Hereford thrown in for variety. On Leap Year day, February 29, the locomotive took the 1A01 19.22 Penzance - Paddington Travelling Post Office (TPO).

Data available in the first week of March revealed 50050 had accumulated 1,264 hours work in the seven months since its F-exam in summer 1987. This was equivalent to an annual average of 2,166 - above average for the fleet but not as productive as some of the other locomotives that received F-exams around the same time. Top marks on that score went to 50028 and 50007. With the highest overall hours (8,199), 50019 looked like the next

withdrawal candidate but it was running an engine not yet one year old, making 50013 and 50047 the most endangered locomotives - each having clocked up over 7,000 hours. Neither lasted very long in traffic and after suffering failures both were condemned in April. The release of 50003 from Laira in early March confirmed the end of classified overhauls for the Class 50 fleet.

One of the highlights of 1988 for Class 50 fans was the chance (three actually!) to experience haulage over the locomotives' original London Midland stamping ground, the Northern section of the WCML. In January the *Fellsman* tour from Taunton to Carlisle running outwards via Shap with a return via Settle had been heavily over-subscribed leading to a repeat being organised for Saturday 23 April. Both were advertised as featuring haulage by double-headed Class 50s and for the second run Bristol Bath Road depot produced the revised NSE liveried duo of 50024 and 50050. The January trip suffered a delay at Gloucester while 50036 *Victorious*, which had refused to work properly with 50008 *Thunderer*, was changed for 50034. This mixed liveried pair then spent the rest of the day clawing back lost time, culminating in a storming

50050 enters Paignton station with the stock for the 10.25 to Paddington on 3 September 1988. *Ian Horner*

It's not everyday that a pair of Network SouthEast liveried Class 50s can be seen at the head of a train on the Settle and Carlisle line at Ribblehead. 50024 *Vanguard* and 50050 *Fearless* stop for an organised photo-call during 'The Fellsman II' tour on 23 April 1988.
Peter Goodman

run over the Cumbrian Fells.

Motive power problems also dogged the repeat run, something which became blatantly obvious as the train tackled the Lickey Incline. To say it was embarrassing would be a master of understatement as a ridiculous 13 minutes were required to cover the two miles uphill section from Bromsgrove to the summit at Blackwell - passed at the funereal pace of 4mph. Prime reason for the slow running was the lack of effort from 50024, but an up to scratch 50050 would surely have been able to lug the complete train (10 coaches for 350 tons) along a little quicker? The chance to drop off the errant 50024 at Birmingham New Street was not taken, leaving 50050, described years later on an internet chat forum as "never the fastest pony in the stable" to continue on without assistance.

North of Birmingham, the 1Z41 05.00 Taunton - Carlisle struggled for pace at times and only made 76mph at Whitmore before racing up to 97mph on the downgrades towards Crewe. This trend would continue through the day, making heavy weather on the gradients followed by high speeds down the slopes where possible.

In the early 1970s the time allowed for a 12 coach train headed by two Class 50s from Carnforth to Shap Summit was 23½ minutes, at an average speed of 81.9mph. Today, unchecked by out of course speed restrictions and hauling two coaches fewer, 50050/024 required an extra six minutes, struggling along at 63.6mph. Shap Summit was conquered at just below 35mph. North of Penrith, the driver allowed his steeds a brief taste of face saving 'ton-up' running as

Southwaite passed by in a red, white and blue blur at 103mph. If nothing else, this performance showed why the Class 50s were so unloved by many on the LMR and not overly missed after their transfer to the WR.

When working well the class was nothing short of brilliant, again as witnessed in contemporary locomotive performance articles published in *The Railway Magazine* (they got top reviews on the Western too!). Poor availability had however, led to trains booked for a pair running with a single locomotive, but the performance of the solo engine was often so good that running one locomotive short became a much easier option in future.

The third 1988 WCML trip ran on Cup Final day in May, taking 50009 and 50036 through to Glasgow

Central - a legendary run that absolutely restored the reputation of the Class 50 on the WCML, and some.

As expected, a squadron of new generation 'Sprinter' type DMUs moved into the south west for the start of the new timetable from Monday 16 May. This in theory consigned the sometimes extraordinary locomotive-hauled local workings in Devon and Cornwall to the history books - in theory. In the final week before the changeover, 50050 hauled the 1C09 06.35 Bristol - Plymouth with 50028 (which was detached at Exeter) on 12 May before taking the 2C83 09.11 Penzance - Plymouth the following day.

A few days later, all such workings were covered by Class 155 DMUs. 50050 meanwhile continued with a month long local restriction, finding work on other largely non passenger trains such as the 1E06 14.15 Plymouth - Leeds van train. By mid June however, the locomotive was back on the Waterloo route, pretty much its

home for the next two months.

At the time all NSE Class 50s were given the same pool code NXXA, regardless of whether allocated to OC or LA depots. There were nine daily diagrams on the Waterloo route but only nine Laira based NSE '50s' - suggesting a need for 100% availability. Thus the official pool was supplemented by locomotives from other sectors such as 50003/043/048/050 (RXXA - parcels) and 50027 (FXXL - freight) all of which looked the part anyhow due to wearing the revised NSE livery.

In early June, 50021 *Rodney* was transferred from OC to LA and assigned to pool NSSA, which would eventually become the LA based Waterloo line pool. In truth however, it hardly touched the Waterloo line all summer and continued to work as if still based at OC. At the weekend, summer Saturday turns continued to take Class 50s to holiday destinations, such as Paignton and Penzance, on trains from Paddington as well as the cross-country route. The

locomotives were typically drawn from all the business sectors and this was probably the final period of regular go anywhere Class 50 services.

Another blow to the long term survival prospects of the Class 50 fleet landed over the second weekend of July as the conveyance of newspaper traffic by rail came to an end. Ultimately it was BR who pulled the plug after business was lost following the recent News International 'Wapping' disputes. BR found that the operation of the remaining traffic just wasn't worth the diminished revenue and opted to cut its losses. The end of such traffic not only left the '50s' with less work to do, but released more Class 47s from similar duties elsewhere, making them available to come south if required.

The last Class 50 hauled newspaper train, the 1V01 01.35 Waterloo - Yeovil Junction departed on Sunday 10 July behind 50050, but as this train also conveyed passengers it remained

First of the last

in the timetable. The ensuing reorganisation of locomotive pools saw the RXXA pool reduced from seven to two as; 50003 (to NSSA), 50005 (DCWA), 50022 (FAWC then DCWA, then scrap), 50043 (NSSA) and 50048 (DCWA then NSSA) moved on. This left 50046 and 50050 in the RXXA pool, kept on to cover the Great Western TPO, which for now remained booked for Class 50 traction.

Summer saw more problems as the planned reduction in Class 50 numbers had led to a smaller pool of spares being available. The '50s' were still needed in service and the fleet size remained greater than the traction plan had supposed and spares supply became an issue.

The situation was not helped by a number of engine failures, some of which had only recently been installed. 50027, outshopped just after Christmas, received a new engine in June after its own had failed twice, while 50028 (new engine installed in September 1987) failed on 1 June and would not work again until November, due to waiting for a replacement engine. Also sitting out the summer at Laira was 50023 - again for the want of a new engine. The power unit fitted inside 50023 dated back to April 1984 after previously being used by 50019 and was due for replacement. Demand for overhauled power units was exceeding the NSE contracted rate of supply after replacements had already been dropped into 50009 and 50041 during May. Crewe works just couldn't keep up.

With 50023 of OC laid up for the

The view from the train as 50050 and 50024 approach Shap Summit whilst working 'The Fellsman II' tour on 23 April 1988. *Andy Inkster*

summer, the London depot had a traction problem with 11 daily NSE turns to cover from its fleet of 15 Class 50s. In addition, 50039 *Implacable* having only recently returned to traffic after spending six months on the sidelines now needed an E-exam, and 50038 - literally on its last legs, was of little help to anyone. Assistance from Devon arrived with 50021 pretty much working as it did before its move west and 50050, which worked as if OC based from the middle of August.

Three more '50s' condemned by the end of September; 50010/022/038 reduced the fleet size to a more manageable 42, helping to ease the spares situation a little as the winter 1988/89 timetable commenced on Monday 4 October. The active fleet still numbered somewhat more than had been envisaged however, given BR's continued position that the class did not have a long term future. This view would be subject to revision over the next couple of years as more ETH fitted Type 4 locomotives were needed than previously planned. Class 50s continued to clock up TOPS hours and approach 'overhaul' time, but withdrawals actually slowed down and over the next 18 months only five more '50s' were condemned. Another fleet reshuffle in

October saw 50046 and 50050 re-housed at Old Oak Common depot. This increased the OC pool to 16 and with the new arrivals being relatively early in their overhaul cycle, injected some youth into the London fleet. The winter timetable called for 11 Capital Class 50s in traffic daily from a fleet of 16 (69%) - the main change being the loss of TPO traffic. Following a reorganisation, all such trains on the Western Region were now diagrammed for Class 47s. Over on the Waterloo route, three '47s' were tried out working alongside the '50s' but this experiment was not continued beyond the next timetable change.

After spending a large chunk of October out of service at OC, 50050 enjoyed a good run in traffic lasting right up to the Christmas holiday. Aside from a visit to Penzance on the 1C04 00.30 Paddington - Penzance in early November, the locomotive worked exclusively on Thames & Chilterns (T&C) duties. This period included three double-headed appearances on the Saturday morning 1F12 10.15 Paddington - Oxford, which was not booked for a pair but regularly produced one. Partners were 50040 (12 November), 50032 *Courageous* (26 November) and 50024 (10 December - to Reading

Adding a splash of colour to the Cumbrian landscape, 50024 *Vanguard* and 50050 *Fearless* head south through Smardale whilst working 'The Fellsman II' tour.
Neil Harvey

only). On 12 November, 50040/050 returned to London on the midday service still in multiple.

At the close of 1988, 50050 had reached 2,911 TOPS hours in the 17 months since its last classified overhaul at Laira, with 2,091 clocked up during 1988. This made 50050 the 12th most productive '50' during the year - again a little lower down the order than it should have been bearing in mind it's still fairly recent F-exam. Top of the charts were 50019 (2,460 hours) followed by 50002/008/027 (all LA based), with 50034 next up claiming top dog status at OC. The performance of 50008 looked particularly noteworthy some 33 months on from its last overhaul. After a solid year mainly working the Waterloo route without too much fuss, 50008 now found itself reduced to lighter duties in the Western Region Civil Engineer's locomotive fleet (DCWA pool). Average accumulated hours across

the whole operational fleet now stood at 5,000.

BR traction strategy plans published as recently as spring 1988 envisaged the reduction of the Class 50 fleet to 38 locomotives by the end of the 1988/89 year. The condemning of 50012 in January reduced the fleet to 41 but three more would have to go soon if this target was to be met. There was still plenty of work for the '50s' however, despite recently being made surplus to the requirements of Inter-City, Provincial and Parcels sectors. A new general shortage of Type 4 traction particularly that capable of supplying ETH however, reduced options for further large-scale dumping of the Class 50s.

For the next two years or so then, the '50s' would be needed but in what numbers was far from clear. Overhauls had ceased, but the 41 locomotives remaining in service

continued racing towards overhauls there was no money to pay for. In addition, spares availability had been reduced, in expectation of a smaller fleet to supply. That left the choice of more withdrawals to increase spares supply or keeping a larger fleet with reduced spares support. It also had to be considered whether switching well-worn components between locomotives was really going to contribute much to reliability beyond the very short term? In early 1989, the established Class 50 interest groups began to consider turning their attentions to preservation, and the Fifty Fund was born.

In December 1988, British Rail's latest traction crisis led to an unexpected and sudden need for additional locomotive-hauled trains. One of the new Class 155 'Sprinter' trains encountered a door fault while in passenger service. Being a safety related incident, the whole fleet was taken

First of the last

out of service straight away for detailed examination (under warranty) resulting in a plethora of locomotive-hauled trains being hastily cobbled together. Class 50s usually drawn from the DCWA pool initially covered a daily diagram taking in Swindon, Weston Super Mare, Penzance and Cardiff but soon all manner of local passenger workings became commonplace.

After re-emerging from OC in the New Year, 50050 continued to work well in regular daily passenger service. As would be expected, the vast majority of turns worked were between Paddington and Newbury or Oxford. Locomotive allocation was now far stricter than previously and OC and LA machines tended in the main to stick to their own diagrams. Friday 6 January saw 50050 work through to Plymouth on the 14.20 from Paddington, with a return being made on Sunday evening with the 17.55.

The following Saturday saw more double-heading on the 10.15 from Paddington as an on-test 50050 teamed up with 50040, returning from Oxford together on the midday service. All must have been fine as the locomotive was quickly returned to normal duties. On 11 February, after working an additional service from Paddington to Newbury Racecourse and back, 50050 made another westward venture when it took the 1C73 19.37 Paddington - Exeter. This train ran via Castle Cary and Yeovil Junction due to engineering work and returned as an empty stock working to Old Oak Common on Sunday morning.

An interesting period of operation began on Saturday 25 February,

when 50036/050 worked the 1F02 08.15 Paddington - Oxford and 1F39 10.00 return, the double-heading due to 50036 being on test following repairs at OC. 50050 continued alone with a return to Newbury before taking the 1B46 17.02 Paddington - Hereford. The next day it returned to London with the 1A65 16.15 from Hereford and Monday and Tuesday saw a return to regular T&C duties. On Wednesday 50050 made for Birmingham New Street on the 1M20 09.40 from Paddington, but instead of returning to London it took over a Manchester to Plymouth service and headed back to its former home in Devon. From 1 March, 50050 rolled back the years as it worked the 1S85 07.07 Plymouth - Glasgow to Birmingham New Street, before doubling back on the 1V59 07.20 Glasgow - Penzance after relieving electric traction in the Midlands. Return to London was made at the head of the 'Up Midnight' through to Paddington. 3 March saw another Saturday evening run down to Exeter heading the 19.37 from Paddington.

A most varied March continued the following weekend when 50050 worked the 1C28 10.02 Paddington - Plymouth (via Badminton) and 1A78 16.20 Plymouth - Paddington return on the 12th. Five days later it made a rare appearance at Waterloo, to take charge of the 09.10 to Exeter. On 23 March 50050 worked in place of a Class 47 on the 1C69 18.07 Paddington - Taunton and 2A51 22.10 Taunton - Bath services. On Sunday 2 April, the 10.02 from Paddington produced 50050 once again, this time in multiple with 50039. At Plymouth the locomotives were split before returning to London via different routes; 50050 headed back to Paddington on the 16.20 while 50039 began a few days on the Southern by hauling empty stock to Exeter and taking the 18.22 to Waterloo.

During February and March a number of OC Class 50s made occasional forays on the Waterloo route as cover for unavailable LA machines. This worked in reverse occasionally also, but generally the Devon fleet needed more helping out than the London fleet. On normal weekdays, the furthest most London based Class 50s ventured was the West Midlands, on turn 201. This was an out and back duty from OC taking in Westbury, Birmingham New Street and finally a late evening trip out to Oxford covering a modest 430 LTM. The 'sprinter' replacement diagram was by now usually worked by an LA based NSE locomotive.

The May 1989 timetable was significant in that it was the final time that booked Class 50 passenger duties actually increased. In spite of perceived unreliability, the EE '50s' took over all duties on the West of England route from Waterloo including the local services to Salisbury, which had hitherto been worked by Class 33/1s and 4TC stock. This increased the locomotive pool for such duties (now coded NSSA) to 20, all of which were based at LA. The seven extra '50s' joining the NSSA pool were selected by the NSE fleet engineer and included 50030 and 50050 from NWRA. The other five - 50005/007/009/016/045, were taken from the DCWA pool to make a full allocation of; 50001/002/003/005/007/009/016/017/018/027/028/029/030/041/043/044/045/048/049/050. A noteworthy inclusion in the fleet was 50049, having been reconverted back to a standard '50/0' at Laira depot in March. All except 50007 (green) and 50009/016/045 (large logo) carried one version or another of NSE red, white and blue livery. The new roster called for 13 locomotives per day, an availability of 65%. Back at OC, Class 47s cascaded from Scotland and Stratford reduced the Class 50 requirement to 11 locomotives (NRWA pool) for seven daily turns.

The three Class 47s allocated to the Waterloo line last October had proven slightly more reliable than the '50s', after recovering from a poor start when failures were common. A shorter range due to lower fuel capacity had caused operational problems however, with locomotives having to be watched carefully and swapped mid-diagram. Brake wear was also harder than on the '50s' - a particular problem on a route known for its strain on brakes. On the route, the '50s' were slightly quicker especially on the re-starts, but not hugely so and both types worked to the same schedules.

The decision to persevere with '50s' in favour of '47s' was primarily due to insufficient twin tanked long range '47s' being available at the time. Ex-Eastfield depot based push-pull machines 47705 and 47714 - with extended fuel capacity - were now based

at OC, but reinforcements could not be expected until May 1990.

A mixed fleet of '47s' and '50s' was deemed the worst case scenario, so for the time being the Class 50s held sway, but in the absence of classified overhauls, how much longer could they hold out? Mid-term, NSE favoured retaining Class 50s over Class 47s on the Waterloo route due to their higher running costs, which strengthened the case for long term investment in the Class 159 DMU. No further withdrawals were expected during the upcoming summer period.

The transfer of 50050 from OC back to LA was facilitated by means of the 1C02 00.05 Paddington - Penzance, which it took as far as Plymouth in the early hours of Saturday 13 May. After a brief call at Laira depot, 50050 worked light to Exeter before going straight into service on the 14.17 to Waterloo. On Sunday night, the 2O05 21.00 Exeter - Salisbury was

double-headed by 50005/050 as a means of getting 50005 on to the route for Monday morning, when the new service would commence. Day one saw 50050 work three trips between Salisbury and Waterloo before taking the 1V16 17.05 to Exeter (turn 227). Next morning the failure of 47547 at Exeter left the 06.45 to Waterloo without any traction - until 50050 answered the call.

The summer timetable at weekends continued to require additional locomotive-hauled trains down to Devon and Cornwall. By 1989 however, the '50s' were left with just three such turns and the season began poorly on Saturday 20 May as only one actually produced, with the very lively 50032 heading the 1C09 06.25 Paddington - Paignton. Fortunately for the 'bashers', 50050 piloted the 08.17 from Paddington (a Class 47 turn) as far as Exeter in tandem with the booked Class 47/7. The Class 50 immediately worked the 1O36 11.50 Exeter - Waterloo starting

50050 passes a Class 47 at Paignton on 3 September 1988.

Ian Horner

50050 starts away from Paddington with the 15.15 service to Oxford, passing 50034 *Furious* which was about to work an empty coaching stock train to Old Oak Common on 27 March 1989.   *Ian Horner*

another sustained period of working through to mid-June when it retired to Laira for maintenance.

On completion of maintenance repairs, 50050 returned to the fray on 24 June when it worked the 1O86 09.33 Plymouth - Brighton as far as Exeter, in multiple with 50045. The 'in traffic' status of the rest of the fleet the same morning was; NSSA 16 of 20 in traffic (80%), DCWA seven of ten (70%) and NWRA six of ten (60%) giving an overall availability of 73%. 50030 of LA had been working off OC all week and continued its run on T&C duties by taking the 1C09 06.25 Paddington - Paignton and 1A40 10.20 return.

After arriving at Exeter on 1O86, 50045 continued onwards alone and 50050 became the spare locomotive. On Sunday morning it worked the 09.28 to Waterloo

before appearing on Thames Valley duties the following Tuesday. By the end of the week it was back on the Waterloo route where it would be practically ever present for the next month.

The new timetable featured a level of double-heading not seen since 1974. This was in part due to the remoteness of Laira depot from the Waterloo route and the need to work locomotives to and from their home depot for scheduled maintenance and repairs. Often a recently repaired spare Class 50 would be sent straight into service in multiple with a classmate just to get it nearer where it might be needed next. The 2C08 07.12 Newton Abbot - Exeter became a regular double-header with the additional locomotive stabled ready to replace another if it was needed. Sometimes the pair would also work the 1O48 08.11 Exeter - Waterloo to get more power up to Salisbury or London. In the

opposite direction, the 5V17 20.48 Exeter - Laira Carriage Sidings regularly produced two Class 50s, as locomotives were worked back to Laira for exams or repairs. Less common for a pair, was the 1O38 14.22 Exeter - Waterloo, which produced 50017/050 as far as Salisbury on 10 July.

Problems occurred for 50050 on Friday 28 July when it failed at Basingstoke following a traction motor flashover. After being removed from the train, it was dragged to Reading depot where it languished for three days before being towed to Old Oak Common at the end of July.

Availability was poor in August with the LA fleet often down to half strength, putting only ten Class 50s into daily traffic. As maintenance staff took their summer breaks, the HST fleet suffered in the heat and Class 50s were not top priority (LA was an

Inter-City depot). Just at the wrong time a number of locomotives became due for heavy exams resulting in increased appearances by '47s' and OC based '50s' on the Waterloo route. Meanwhile NSSA pool Class 50s - 50002 and 50043 continued to suffer chronic reliability problems throughout the whole year. In addition to locomotive shortages the Waterloo route was often short of coaches too, with reduced formations increasingly common. This was mitigated to an extent by the use of 4TC sets (previously used with Class 33/1s) on the Salisbury and Yeovil workings.

As summer wore on, the OC fleet had its problems too. Down to ten locomotives since 50039 was put out of its misery in June, the London '50s' had gained a reputation for reliability and high availability in spite of their much higher accumulated TOPS hours. This confirmed the benefit of much easier diagrams with lower daily mileages, fewer station stops and nearly all turns starting and finishing at OC depot. Availability began to suffer in August however, with 50023 already sidelined primarily for a full repaint (apparently after being noted in poor external state by NSE management), and compounded further when 50025 derailed at relatively high speed between Hanwell and West Ealing on 6 August.

Investigations quickly found vandalism as the cause but in spite of a reward being offered, nobody was ever charged. The damage to 50025 didn't look any worse than that suffered by 50041 in 1983, but this was 1989 and it was quickly decided to withdraw the locomotive and increase the spares pool. Two days after the derailment, the OC fleet was down to five working '50s' from the nine left. With 50026 out of service due to engine problems, about to be

joined by 50024, and 50031 *Hood* coming up for a D-exam, the staff at OC had their work cut out.

Entering the second week of August, 50050's TOPS hours stood at 4,112 - an increase of 1,201 since the turn of the year. This made it the sixth most productive Class 50 of the year so far. Current top performer this year was the incredible 50041, which had run 1,632 hours - nearly 36% more than 50050. While this was an exceptional performance, more normal would be the scores posted by 50003/028/048 (between 1,330 and 1,429 hours). All but two of the top 13 performers were LA based. Quickest out of the blocks since the latest timetable change were 50041/029/009, all comfortably clear of next best 50007.

After returning from its latest period of downtime in early August, 50050 was noted in traffic with one of its bodyside crests missing. Thefts of the attractive Royal Navy crests had long been a problem, with those presented to 50025 being missing for years. The other crest would eventually be removed from 50050 for safe keeping until it was refitted for a short time in 1994.

Workings remained primarily on the Waterloo route but on 21 August 50050 enjoyed a return to past glories. After working into Paddington with the 06.52 from Westbury, *Fearless* worked the 1C60 15.38 Paddington - Plymouth back home to Devon. The next day it was business as usual on the 1O32 06.45 Exeter - Waterloo. September saw more double-heading and more trouble. On the 6th, 50050 worked the 2V05 05.57 Salisbury - Exeter, but instead of working the 10.20 to Waterloo, it was sent to Laira for attention by way of the 18.20 Exeter Riverside - Tavistock Junction departmental trip - in the company of 50019. On Friday the

15th after working up to Waterloo on the 05.56 from Exeter, *Fearless* failed to re-start its engine and could not take the 11.15 to Exeter. Revived at Old Oak Common the next day, 50050 was turned out for the 17.40 Paddington - Cheltenham Spa on Saturday evening and was back at Waterloo in time to take the 06.52 to Exeter on Monday 18 September.

Late September saw more time out of traffic. On the 25th, 50050 again worked the 2V05 05.57 Salisbury - Exeter (with 50044) for transfer to Laira rather than taking the next Waterloo train. Movement was made by 50020 hauling three dead '50s' (50001/030/050). Two days later 50030 and 50050 worked light to Exeter, but while 50030 went back into passenger service, 50050 returned to depot, this time with 50008. On 29 September and seemingly back in good health, 50050 worked the 2C08 07.12 Newton Abbot - Exeter and 08.11 Exeter - Waterloo, both in multiple with 50018.

The Class 50 fleet size remained at 39 - one more than was planned five months previously, and the last one down (50025) was written off early, hardly a normal withdrawal. DCWA allocated 50040 had languished at LA requiring a new engine and bogies since late August but it had not been condemned. At OC, 50039 which had been withdrawn in June was inspected with a view to assessment of reinstatement costs - were the '50s' still wanted? If the answer was yes, this was not backed up with the promise of more overhauls. As the expected delivery dates of new generation DMU stock fell further behind schedule however, the view that BR needed more passenger train

On 4 July 1989, 50050 speeds through Worting Junction on the 17.05 Waterloo - Exeter.

Bob Foster

locomotives than previously thought gained further credence.

The winter 1989 locomotive rosters changed little from the summer at LA, but the arrival of additional Class 47s at OC increased their daily NSE diagrams to six. Class 50s and '47s' would be expected to work alongside each other on Thames Valley duties until May 1990, when more displaced Sulzers cascaded from other depots would become available. From then on, the '47s' would take full control until NSE received its new Class 165/166 'Turbo' DMUs. This left the OC '50s' with seven daily diagrams to cover from a fleet of nine aged locomotives (77% availability), demonstrating once again that BR always asked a lot from the '50s'.

The first week of October saw 50050 working to its usual diet of Waterloo to Exeter services, including double-heading in Devon with 50041 on 3 October and 50027 the following day. There was little change to the routine until mid-November when 50050 hauled the afternoon Plymouth to Leeds vans as far as Gloucester, before heading for home on the corresponding working from Newcastle. 21 November saw 50050 join up with 50015 *Valiant* to work the 14.30 Tavistock Junction - Exeter Riverside departmental trip. These workings suggest 50050 was being kept local at the time, but two days later it was back on NSE duties.

More double-heading was to be had on the Waterloo route in early December before 50050 moved across to the Thames Valley for the weekend of 9 and 10 December. Then on Thursday 14 December, 50029/050 worked 1O31 05.56 Exeter - Waterloo and 1V11 11.15 Waterloo - Exeter throughout - the newly repainted 50029 (in dark blue NSE livery) being on test following its latest engine change. With 5,400 bhp and a keen driver, the pair made little effort of the climb from Andover and hammered over the summit just past Grateley station at 90mph.

The final months of 1989 saw no further Class 50s withdrawn from service, but the expected condemning of 50040 was confirmed in early November. Surprisingly 50040's status was updated to "stored unserviceable" 24 hours later, and it kept its place among the surviving fleet members − in theory at least. In mid-December, another DCWA machine, 50021 was stopped at LA in need of engine repairs but like 50040 would ultimately never work again. Analysis of accumulated hours for the 39 remaining locomotives on 31 December revealed the average per locomotive was now 6,618 with 1,654 each being added over the previous 12 months.

The life & times of 50050 *Fearless*

Top scorer in 1989 by a long way was 50041, which in spite of its high overall total hours (10,366) was running an engine installed as recently as May 1988. This helped *Bulwark* rack up 2,629 hours over the year, 332 more than the nearest challenger 50003. Having just cleared 5,000 total accumulated hours, 50050 was the fifth most productive in 1989 with 2,158 over the year. The vast majority of the top performers continued to be LA based.

For all its heroics the previous year, it all went sour for 50041 in the early days of 1990 when it suffered a main generator failure. Following a repair at LA it failed again on test and the locomotive joined 50005 and 50037 in the queue for a new main generator. The most notable working for 50050 in early 1990 occurred on February 15 when flooding of the railway line east of Exeter led to an emergency timetable being put into place. *Fearless* took the opportunity for an away day from

the Waterloo line as it hauled the 15.26 Exeter - Penzance and 20.10 Penzance - Plymouth.

50050 sat out March 1990 at Laira depot undergoing an E-exam, and once again it had been kept in service beyond 5,000 hours.

During 1990, 15 Class 50s were withdrawn from service starting with 50021 (DCWA) and 50041 (NSSA) - condemned on the same day in mid April. This left the NSSA fleet one '50' short while a replacement was nominated. Soon after, 50004 (DCWA) and 50034 (NWRA) suffered major failures, leading to both being condemned in June. A plan to make one good locomotive from the pair was aborted when it became clear that there was no point as more withdrawals were coming.

The May 1990 timetable change came and went, but a handful of '50s' remained in traffic for NSE based at OC depot. There was even one remaining weekend turn to Paignton, which unsurprisingly

proved popular with the 'bashers'. At the end of May, 50031/032/034/036 were transferred to Laira (DCWA pool) leaving a final quintet; 50023/024/026/033/035 based at OC. In early July however, and driven more by chronic availability of the LA Class 50 fleet as much as the arrival of additional Class 47s, the remaining Old Oak '50s' moved to Laira. The NSE locomotive pool was now coded NWXA, with a separate pool (NWXC) created for reserves.

Halfway through the year and with 15 Class 50s now taken out of traffic for good, the remaining 35 (including 50040) were left to struggle on, barely aided by an increase in spare parts robbed from former stable mates. Of the survivors, many had already passed 8,000 hours - the normal shopping interval for classified overhauls, suggesting reliability and availability was not about to improve anytime soon. Having just cleared 6,300 hours 50050 had been the sixth most productive

50050 snakes its way into the familiar surroundings of Waterloo station, having worked the 11.50 Exeter - Waterloo on 20 May 1989.
Ian Horner

First of the last

13 August and 50050 stands at Salisbury station, with 50033 *Glorious* and 50007 *Sir Edward Elgar* alongside. Three days later the locomotive returned to this location following a main generator failure and had to be towed back to Laira and an uncertain future. Thankfully, all three of these locomotives survived and went on to become Laira's railtour trio.

Ian Horner

Class 50 of the year so far, but at its current rate of progress would become due for its next overhaul or withdrawal in spring 1991.

July 1990, saw 50050 make two visits to Paignton, one each by Inter-City and NSE services. On Sunday the 15th, 50026/050 worked the 2C08 09.40 Plymouth - Paignton and 1O37 11.05 Paignton - Waterloo, as far as Exeter. Unfortunately 50050's engine shut down on departure from Newton Abbot on the second run but was re-started at Starcross station.

On Saturday 28 July, the 1C13 08.02 Paddington - Paignton (a Class 47 turn) required a locomotive change at Exeter St David's and 50050 was provided to work the final few miles to the English Riviera resort. 50050 had worked down to Laira depot the

previous night on the 5V17 ECS (with 50007) before returning to Exeter the next morning. After running round the lightweight formation of air-conditioned stock in Goodrington Sidings, *Fearless* then worked the 1A65 13.24 Paignton - Paddington back to Exeter St David's, where it was replaced by 50044 for a fast run on to London.

The early days of August saw 50050 in regular action on the Waterloo route, with only the occasional double-header breaking the monotony of the same scenery day after day. The middle of the month however, brought trouble and big trouble at that.

On Thursday 16 August, 50050 was allocated to turn 230 and left Laira Carriage Sidings at around 04.55 with the 2C99 staff train to Exeter St David's. After running

round, the locomotive continued with the 1O32 06.45 Waterloo service but didn't make it to London due suffering a main generator flashover at Wilton, just short of Salisbury. 50033 was despatched to haul the delinquent into Salisbury station where it was dumped in the bay platform on the down side of the station.

The locomotive was towed back home the same night by 50017. This was achieved by conveying the failed 50050 'dead in train' on the 1V19 19.15 Waterloo - Exeter, from Salisbury (50017 and silent friend replacing 50045) and subsequent 5V19 empty stock train to Laira. Arrival back at the depot was timed at just after midnight. Nobody quite knew it at the time, but it would be seven months before *Fearless* hauled a passenger train again.

Fearless

First of the last

50050 Fearless

The life & times of *50050 Fearless*

Network SouthEast

Above: 50050 & 50045 *Achilles* run alongside the famous sea wall at Dawlish with a Plymouth to Brighton working on 24 June 1989.　　　*Paul Winter*

Left: *Fearless* stands at Salisbury.　　　*Steve Kemp*

Below: 50050 runs through Dawlish Warren with the 10.25 Paignton - Paddington on 3 September 1988.
　　　Peter Goodman

Opposite Page Bottom: 50026 *Indomitable* and 50050 run round their train at Newton Abbot, whilst working the 09.40 Plymouth - Paignton on 15 July 1990.
　　　Peter Goodman

50050 Fearless

Above: A wonderful night study of 50050 at Exeter St Davids at the head of a mail train on 26 July 1988.
Nigel Cockburn

Right: 50050 stands at Penzance at the head of a train to Plymouth on 8 November 1988. *Greg Edwards*

Across the five timetable periods covering summer 1984-86 inclusive, the daily Paddington to Paignton 'Torbay Express' returned to locomotive haulage - diagrammed for a Class 50. The train was usually formed of nine Mk 2 coaches, the majority of which were air-conditioned.

On a morning blessed by bright winter sunshine, 50050 led its train away from Platform Two at Paddington and headed straight for the down main line. Passing the since-closed Westbourne Park station in around two and a quarter minutes boded well for a good run to Reading.

Getting well stuck in at Acton Main Line, speed rose steadily up to the maximum permitted for both locomotive and rolling stock just after Langley station. On some days, 100mph running was thwarted by the presence of a 90mph restricted General Utility Van in the formation - but not today. Beyond Slough, on the slightly adverse grade, speed was held easily in the high 90s mph before passing Twyford in 22 minutes - two minutes ahead of the schedule (for a Class 47 and nine coaches, dated summer 2001).

The five minutes allowed from Twyford to the stop at Reading included one minute for engineering work - [1]. This made the net schedule (full schedule minus allowances), just four minutes. On his unchecked approach to Reading today however, the driver used an additional half a minute to ensure a smooth arrival at the platform, a trait repeated throughout the journey. His colleagues were not always so considerate!

Between Reading and Westbury, the schedule is that applicable to a Class 47 and seven coaches, also from the summer of 2001. With the heavier load, 50050 failed to match the 15 minutes allowed to Newbury by just two seconds. Back in 1985, the speed restriction for the left hand curve through Hungerford was just 60mph, which in turn limited speed gain through Bedwyn before the brakes were applied for Crofton Curve. This would not fully explain the loss of two minutes on the 2001 schedule to Pewsey however, and this section was covered in a time slower than was typical of the time. Sustained high speed running across the Vale of Pewsey ensured a good showing from 50050 against the lighter 2001 schedule as it passed Lavington. A long standing TSR at Heywood Road Junction however, blighted the final approach to Westbury station - adding one minute to the potential time.

The section from Westbury to Witham (East Somerset) Junction often rode badly and was particularly vulnerable to TSRs. With no such formal handicaps evident today, 50050 was nevertheless taken steadily on the Frome avoider, before being opened up after passing the junction for Merehead Quarry. Disappointing then that the fast

50050 *Fearless* stands at Exeter St Davids on 16 February 1985 after hauling 1C32 from London Paddington, as detailed on these pages.
Andy Inkster

First of the last

swooping section down to Bruton would be blighted by a slowing to 30mph, just as the pace ought to have been quickening! West of Castle Cary, line speed of 90mph was reached and held easily with a slight excess near East Langport being quickly reigned in. The schedule quoted here is current and seemingly quite generous. It does however, include a pathing allowance approaching Taunton and is timed for a heavier load.

Restarting westbound from Taunton always called for maximum effort from the locomotive, and 50050's driver took his train away smartly, quickly building speed up to Wellington. Once on the slope proper towards Whiteball Summit, *Fearless* performed exceptionally well as it worked at full power with speed falling against the grade - not circumstances to view the Class 50 at its best. Minimum speed in the tunnel was not recorded, put to pass the summit at 69mph with nine mainly air-conditioned coaches on, highlighted a locomotive on top form - with power output significantly exceeding the 2,700bhp normal service rating of the 16CSVT engine. Such performances were common in Class 50s at the time, for reasons eloquently set out in *Class 50s in Operation*.

Once into Devon, 1C32 ran easily down the favourable gradients towards Exeter St David's without any unnecessary fast running. West of Taunton, the schedule is again for a Class 47 and nine coaches - against which 50050 compares well at Tiverton Junction. More track improvements since 1985 have lifted the line speed through the Cullompton curves to 100mph. Adverse signals approaching Cowley Bridge Junction, slowed the running time from Taunton to almost half an hour before 50050 pulled up at platform one for a breather in the wintry sunshine. After waiting time at Exeter, the train would continue on to the English Riviera at a slower pace, making five stops in the remaining 28 miles through to Paignton.

Miles	Location	Sched & Allows	Time	Comments / mph
0.0	Paddington	0	00.00	P2
1.1	Westbourne Park		02.16	52
4.2	Acton Main Line		05.01	79
9.0	Southall		08.24	91
10.8	Hayes & Harlington		09.35	93
13.2	West Drayton		11.01	97
16.2	Langley		12.51	98 / 101
18.4	Slough	15	14.10	100
24.2	Maidenhead	19	17.46	96
31.0	Twyford	24 [1]	21.59	97
35.9	Reading	29	26.30	...
1.0	Reading West		01.52	47
5.3	Theale		05.36	...
8.8	Aldermaston		08.00	89
10.8	Midgham		09.18	90
13.6	Thatcham		11.12	89
17.1	Newbury	15	15.02	...
8.5	Hungerford		09.00	60*
13.3	Bedwyn		12.58	82
17.0	Savernake		16.04	73
22.3	Pewsey	19	20.58	...
3.6	Woodborough	4	04.11	85
5.7	Patney		05.38	89
12.8	Lavington	10	10.13	98
16.1	Edington	[2]	12.16	97
19.2	Heywood Road Junction	17	15.25	TSR 20*
20.3	Westbury	19	18.17	...
1.4	Fairwood Junction	3	02.38	38*
4.8	Clink Road Junction	7	06.11	69
6.7	Blatchbridge Junction	9	07.41	73
11.1	East Somerset Junction	12	10.43	83
16.3	Bruton		14.27	89 / TSR 30*
19.8	Castle Cary	20	18.41	62 / 89
30.1	Somerton	27	26.03	86 / 93
39.4	Athelney Level Crossing	33	32.11	90
42.6	Cogload Junction SB	36 (1H)	34.18	88
47.3	Taunton	42	39.51	...
1.3	Silk Mills Level Crossing		02.23	57
7.1	Wellington		07.11	79
10.9	Whiteball Summit (MP 174)		10.18	69
16.0	Tiverton Junction	14H	13.53	83
18.2	Cullompton		15.39	80*
22.4	Hele		18.40	88
27.1	Stoke Canon Level Crossing		22.03	87
29.5	Cowley Bridge Junction	23 [2]	25.45	sigs 20*
30.8	Exeter St David's	27	29.56	...

See page 29 for explanation on performance tables.   * indicates a speed restriction

Saturday 16 February 1985 1C32 10.35 Paddington - Paignton
50050 + 9 x Mk2 Coaches   300/320 tons (air-con)

The life & times of 50050 *Fearless*

Six months after failing with a main generator flashover and with its transformation back to D400 now underway, 50050 stands in the midst of its repaint at Laira depot on 17 February 1991. *Peter Goodman*

Summer 1990 was not the time to be a Class 50 in need of a replacement major component such as a main generator. The previous weeks had seen 50004/ 034/020/016/035 condemned - all needing a new engine or main generator, as the rundown of the fleet continued.

At Laira, scheduled maintenance in the form of E-exams for 50001/ 024/027/028/029 understandably took priority over unclassified repairs - although 50050 was initially shown on TOPS as stopped for a C-exam plus generator repair. The falling of so many heavy exams during a period when many depot fitting staff would be taking time off for holidays could be viewed as unlucky - but then again, some of these exams were well overdue. Criticism 20 years later is easy and

there were probably very good reasons to keep deferring the exams.

Just to add to the pain, 50005 and 50037 both suffered major engine failures at the end of September. The engine block inside 50037 (IH5567) was that which had originally been fitted to the prototype DP2. In October the damaged engine was dumped inside the now-withdrawn 50023, destined never to run again.

For 50050 however, there was a lifeline. Stories had been circulating that NSE might be receptive to a suggestion to repaint the locomotive in original livery for its final year in traffic even before its August failure. The shabby NSE livery applied three years earlier would probably have been reapplied with the darker

blue style sometime in late 1990 - raising the question did it have to be NSE livery?

The idea was soon picked up by *RAIL* magazine who contacted NSE, leading to an appeal being launched to raise funds for the repaint. This quickly captured the imagination of *RAIL* readers who responded immediately with hard cash. The front page of Issue 133 featured an NSE liveried 50050 leading a Waterloo train declaring "D400 the money pours in - Help us put it in blue!" Of course, paintwork aside, there was still the small matter of returning the locomotive to working order. A new main generator arrived at Laira depot in late September apparently for fitting into 50050 but this was prioritised elsewhere. While awaiting attention to be switched its way, 50050 took up

First of the last

residence in the storage sidings beside the main line at Laira - otherwise known as the scrap line.

In October, three Class 50s were withdrawn in full working order; 50023/032/042 (all DCWA pool) were literally switched off. In terms of putting another '50' into traffic, NSE would have been better off taking on 50042 with its recently installed engine (five months old) rather than throw time and money at 50050. This just emphasises how seriously the D400 project was taken. With only 6,478 hours on the clock, 50050 had relative youth on its side compared to the 8,049 run by 50042, but with all the chopping and changing of engines and main generators over the last couple of years, the soundness of judging Class 50 lifespan by TOPS hours accumulated had long since diminished.

During the latter months of 1990, the Waterloo to Exeter line timetable descended into a regular shambles as poor reliability and shortages of rolling stock drove customers and staff alike to despair. NSE Class 50 availability sunk to new lows over Christmas with locomotives from the 'Golden Oldies' DCWA pool being drafted in to assist along with as many Class 33s and '47s' that could be rustled up from other duties. With there being no danger of any money being made available for some more overhauls, NSE waved the white flag and gave notice of a reduced timetable to take effect from Monday 21 January 1991. All this passed 50050 by, as it remained holed up at Laira with no expectation of a return to service soon.

The triple whammy of 50024/028/ 043 receiving their marching orders on the first day of February 1991 reduced the fleet to a mere 19 examples. The DCWA locomotives had by now all been withdrawn or transferred to the passenger pools with the

Two more views of 50050 undergoing its repaint into original blue colours as D400 in February 1991. The repaint created a great deal of interest and was funded following an appeal in *RAIL* magazine.

Peter Goodman

exceptions of the recently repainted 50008 and 50015 - now hanging on as celebrity railtour and open day machines. With spending on the '50s' down to nothing but the bare necessities, and deliveries of the Class 159 DMUs being delayed, NSE now had some tough questions to deal with.

Continuous use on the Waterloo route had stressed the engines and generators of the Class 50s so much that they were failing and

wearing out much sooner than when they worked on varied duties. Even last overhauled 50003, after being one of the top performers in recent years had run into trouble and in its final year of service struggled to record a level of productivity comparable with locomotives from the former DCWA fleet. Crewe Works was still sending overhauled or part overhauled 'half life' engines down to Devon for installation into Class 50s but this proved to be an inadequate

Nearly ready. The repaint back into original BR blue livery is almost complete at Laira Depot on 24 March 1991, with just the D400 numbers to be added.   *Peter Goodman*

substitute for proper overhauls.

On 1 February, a lorry arrived at Laira depot conveying a fully overhauled power unit for use inside 50050. Engine IH6944, first used inside D416 some 23 years earlier, was craned straight into its latest host and attention began to be concentrated on the locomotive's bodywork.

On 28 March, the railway press was invited to Laira to witness the unveiling of the re-born 50050. The '50' looked immaculate in its new coat of BR blue livery, wearing its original identity of D400 under all four cabsides with the BR double arrow symbol - just as it did when brand new in 1967. Well not quite, the orange band carried at cant rail level reminded everyone that it was still 1991. Also present was the railtour duo 50008 and 50015.

D400 had worked a light diesel run to Exeter and back in late March, but its first loaded test run took place on Wednesday 3 April when it joined green liveried 50007 on the 5C08 06.10 Laira - Newton Abbot ECS and 2C08 07.12 Newton Abbot - Exeter local passenger train. Three days

later the big day arrived as D400 was allocated to the 1O86 09.45 Plymouth - Waterloo, which it worked throughout with a train packed with enthusiasts. The gleaming locomotive brightened up a wet day at Waterloo station where a special ceremony marked the re-entry of D400 to service. Some more pedantic observers remarked on the incorrect sized running numbers but this was a small detail - 50050, or D400 was back.

Another Class 50 back into traffic was good news as April saw two more casualties; 50001 and 50036. On Sunday 28 April, a failed Class 47 led to a return to Western Region Inter-City duties for D400, as it hauled the 1A28 10.10 Exeter - Paddington.

The introduction of the summer 1991 timetable was delayed until early July due to the late delivery of the new Mk 4 coaches for use on the recently electrified ECML. This meant the cascade of HSTs

onto additional cross country workings and onward alterations to locomotive-hauled services could not take place until this time. The new timetable would see the end of the wagon load 'Speedlink' freight network rendering scores of locomotives redundant, including a batch of ETH fitted Class 47s based at Tinsley depot (TI). These were to be moved to OC and put into service on NSE duties, spelling the death knell for the remaining Class 50s.

The remaining NSE allocated Class 50s (50002/003/007/017/018/027/029/030/031/033/037/046/048/049/D400) continued in service through May and June with no further locomotives withdrawn from service. Star performer was D400, which appeared daily on the Waterloo route and was highly sought by '50' fans new and old. The front coaches of Class 50 hauled trains were often packed, especially at the weekend as enthusiasts savoured the final few months of operation by NSE.

The final overhauled power unit from Crewe was installed into 50046 during a C-exam in May, setting it up to be one of the most reliable performers throughout the remainder of 1991. Without a full repaint in four years, *Ajax* became a firm favourite as it ran around in its rather tatty 1987 vintage large logo livery complete with a black roof. To commemorate 50 years since H.M.S. *Hood* was sunk by the German battleship *Bismarck*, Laira depot adorned 50031 *Hood* with a new coat of large logo livery - with a grey roof. This ensured 50031 looked smart during its final eight weeks in service.

On 6 April 1991, D400 makes its debut into service following its retro-repaint from 50050. The locomotive pauses at Gillingham, working the 17.15 Waterloo - Exeter.   *Peter Goodman*

July 1991 marked the last time that Class 50s held sway on the Waterloo to Exeter route. As the ex-TI Class 47s made their way to OC, the best of the bunch were put into traffic on Thames Valley passenger duties. This released the recently overhauled Class 47/7s to the tougher Waterloo route and so led to more '50s' being sidelined. Some of the former Speedlink Class 47s were pretty ragged however, and needed work doing at OC before being declared fit for service. This gave the '50s' a brief reprieve on the services. By late July however, Sulzer power was in the ascendancy on both routes.

Five Class 50s were withdrawn in July, including green 50007, which would later be reinstated for railtour use and last-overhauled 50003. Two more fell in August and three in September as the Class 50s were effectively finished with by NSE. Many of those withdrawn at this time were still runners but in need of exams or engine repairs to remain in service. With no money available, there was only going to be one outcome. One of the better ones, 50048 succumbed after colliding with a trespassing herd of cows near Exmouth Junction in mid June.

Spring and summer saw differing fortunes for D400. On 4 May, it took the 2O82 06.45 Exeter - Waterloo throughout with 50048. This enabled the celebrity blue locomotive to attend the open day at Wimbledon depot, held over the bank holiday weekend. On the Tuesday however, D400 was seen arriving at Exeter under tow from two Class 33s. After a few days back in the garage at Laira, it reappeared on the by now famous 07.12 from Newton Abbot double-heading with 50027. Just over a week later, on 21 May the former 50050 was in trouble again as it failed at Crewkerne while in charge of the 16.55 from Waterloo. Rescue was affected by 50029/037 sent up from Exeter. Transfer to Laira was made the following night when 50033 towed 50003 and D400 home.

Another return to traffic was made on Saturday 25 May, when D400 worked the 06.45 and 17.42 from Exeter, split by the 13.15 from Waterloo. This began a good period of service including two Sunday visits to Paignton in June with the 12.20 from Exeter, and 17.35 to Waterloo.

On the last Saturday of June, the first and last built '50s' teamed up to haul the 07.12 from Newton Abbot, splendidly illuminated by the rising sunlight drenching the sea wall section. There were still problems of course, including on 10 July when a small electrical fire halted D400 at Pinhoe on the 06.15 from Salisbury. Arrival at Exeter was nearly one hour late after being towed in by a Class 33, but damage was light and D400

The life & times of 50050 *Fearless*

First and the last: First built D400 double-heads with 50049 *Defiance* on the 07.12 Newton Abbot - Exeter on 29 June 1991, passing underneath the bridge at Teignmouth. The sea wall at Teignmouth and Dawlish provided many wonderful photographic opportunities for railway enthusiasts.   *Ian Horner*

returned to service the same day.

In mid August Old Oak Common depot held another open day with D400 predictably on display. The locomotive then returned to the Waterloo route but failed on Wednesday 21 August, after suffering power unit overloads. The failure was dragged westwards 'dead in train' by a Class 47/7 on the 1V09 08.40 Waterloo - Exeter before spending another six weeks on the sidelines awaiting another power unit. Again had this been any other Class 50, it would surely would have been withdrawn from service? The 'new' power unit was donated by the recently withdrawn 50048, which had used it since its final E-exam in November 1989. Even then the engine was classed as 'half life' (not freshly overhauled) but nevertheless 50048 had since carved a reputation for stellar performance, until minor collision damage

caused its premature withdrawal from service.

On Sunday 15 September Laira depot held an open day too, with the lines of withdrawn Class 50s sadly outnumbering those left in traffic. Even though it was still out of service, the future of D400 was assured (for the next 12 months at least), when Peter Field (NSE's Director for South West services) confirmed it would be kept on for special workings beyond the end of normal Class 50 operations. Another plaque was unveiled on the side of D400 reading "RESTORED TO ORIGINAL LIVERY WITH HELP FROM OUR LOYAL READERS 1991 - RAIL - D400" The editor of *RAIL*, Murray Brown, paid tribute to the efforts of the team at Laira depot for keeping the '50s' going declaring that "no other depot has done more to cater for enthusiasts than Laira".

D400 made its latest return to traffic in early October, just in time to haul an additional 10.00 Waterloo - Exeter 'Network Day' train with 50030 on Saturday 5 October. The blue '50' was entrusted to work the 15.07 return train solo, and continued to behave throughout the rest of the month. As the winter 1991/92 timetable commenced there were still insufficient Class 47 to cover all NSE's requirements and five '50s' (50029/030/033/046/D400) remained active to provide cover. In addition, 'Sunday best' 50008 and 50015 were available at Laira for railtours and other special duties, but they did not work everyday service trains and indeed would haul their final railtour in late November. Also not yet out of the picture was Laira's pet '50', the green liveried 50007 which continued to languish at the depot, but had not been robbed of components to keep other '50s' running, as was normal practice.

On 21 August 1991, 47710 *Capital Radio's Help A London Child* hauls a failed D400 through Stoford. *Martin Loader*

In late 1991, permission was given for Laira depot to return 50007 to service for a programme of special farewell trains planned for the next couple of years - if there was sufficient demand. 50007 had a small problem though - it needed a replacement power unit and bogies. These were controversially supplied from 50046, the top performer in the fleet since its power unit change in May.

In mid November 50046 was stopped at LA for the last time. This took a good performing locomotive out of traffic at a time when the new superior Class 47/7s were struggling along and still in need of assistance from the engines they were replacing. Five days before its final day in passenger service however, 50046 failed at Honiton with a Basingstoke service. Assistance was provided by D400, which later dumped the large logo machine at Waterloo before heading off to Eastleigh.

That left four NSE survivors, which were by now virtual wrecks gamely staggering along to help keep the timetable running. Despite their problems however, 50029/030/D400 covered over 33,000 miles between them during November supplemented by occasional appearances from 50033. The situation spurred NSE into considering reinstating some Class 50s but many, especially the better ones had already been sold or placed on the tender list for sale. There were reports of plans to restore 50017 and 50027 to traffic but nothing ever came about.

Aside from a week off for traction motor flashover repairs in the middle of the month, D400 was virtually ever present throughout November. Just before Christmas however, it failed at Salisbury after suffering low power due to a turbocharger defect. Following repairs at Laira, D400 returned to service on New Year's Eve, joining

50030 at the head of the 07.12 from Newton Abbot before taking over the Plymouth to Waterloo service at Exeter. The early days of 1992 saw continued action on the Waterloo to Exeter line.

The weekend of 18/19 January 1992 was scheduled by NSE to mark the end of Class 50s on its services, with D400 mooted as potential traction for a Thames Valley turn on Friday 17 January. This idea was soon dropped as an army of train spotters at Paddington on a Friday afternoon was deemed not desirable and in any case the '50s' were still needed in normal service. That

same weekend, OC was four Class 47/7s short of the 15 required to cover all the booked turns. The demise of 50029 on 2 January with a seized engine left just three '50s' available to help out.

The first of a number of railtours promoted late the previous year ran on Saturday 25 January - by this time of course, the '50s' should have been consigned to history in normal service. Advertised for a pair, the 'Network Navigator' ran from Birmingham via Bristol and Reading to various places in Sussex and Hampshire. After

D400, alongside 47484 *Isambard Kingdom Brunel* and 31568 on display at the Old Oak Common Open Day on 18 August 1991. *John Neave*

The introduction of NSE 50033 *Glorious* to the dedicated Class 50 railtour fleet brought a more colourful variety to the final couple of years and to mark its new role 50033 was fully repainted into NSE colours in early 1992. 50033 and D400 stand at Chepstow on 4 April 1992 whist working the 'Hoovering Druid' railtour.   *Peter Goodman*

running light from Laira to Bescot the previous night, D400/50030 duly took the 1Z25 06.05 Manchester Piccadilly - Fratton forward from Birmingham, later visiting Littlehampton and Bognor Regis along the way - both locations seeing their first '50s'.

D400 soon returned to Waterloo line duties but not for long. After working the 1V18 17.34 Waterloo

The replica English Electric leasing plate and *RAIL* commemorative plaques, as carried on the side of D400.   *Martin Loader*

- Yeovil Junction and ECS back to Eastleigh on 30 January, it retired to OC with flashover damage. Transfer back home to Laira was made via Bristol Bath Road depot where it resided over the first weekend of February. D400 did not return to traffic until April (on railtour duties), and thus its regular career with British Rail was effectively over. This left just 50030 and 50033 to soldier on until late February and mid March respectively on NSE duties.

On the first Saturday of April, a trip promoted by Pathfinder Tours promised double-headed Class 50 haulage from Derby down to various South Wales branch lines. Joining nominated railtour locomotive D400 would be 50033, but it would need repairs at LA to address a smoking engine beforehand. On Friday 3 April, Laira depot held another

photo-call as the restoration of 50007 was finally completed - nearly five months on from when 50046 worked its last trains. On a fine spring morning, 50033 - which had been freshly repainted in NSE livery, 50007 and D400 posed on adjacent roads for the cameras before D400 and 50033 were prepared for Saturday's outing. To ensure all was in order, the pair was sent on a test run to Newton Abbot and back hauling a set of Royal Mail coaches.

Dubbed the 'Hoovering Druid', the tour was a tale of three thirds as a few hours meandering round Glamorgan and Gwent at very low speeds was sandwiched by some high spirited running from and back to Derby. Outposts visited included Pontycymmer, Margam Abbey Works East and Ebbw Vale South. A fast run home included a rocket propelled ascent of the

Lickey Incline and a brief burst up to 105mph before being eased at Longbridge. Although booked into Birmingham New Street via Selly Oak, 1Z16 was signalled through Camp Hill leaving the train pointing the wrong way for onward travel to Derby. This was solved by running via Selly Oak in the opposite direction to that planned and taking the Lifford Curve before passing Camp Hill for the second time, this time keeping straight ahead to Landor Street Junction and ultimately Derby. This was the last time D400 hauled a passenger train for British Rail at its design speed before being restricted to 75mph to aid reliability.

A week later the rejuvenated 50007 joined D400 to work the 'Carlisle Fifty Farewell' tour from Waterloo to Carlisle, running out and back via Shap. The 1Z38 08.20 Waterloo - Carlisle ran via Barnes to Reading where it departed five minutes late on the down main line. Once 75mph had been reached the locomotives were eased, having had their maximum speeds restricted by Geoff Hudson, the Area Fleet Manager at Laira. This was to reduce the risk of flashover damage, for which there would be no money

available to carry out any arising repairs. Unfortunately, this made the train run late all day as it had been too late to accommodate the reduced maximum speed in the train specification.

The planned photo-stop at Lancaster was still taken however, and thoughts turned to the "Mountain section" ahead and how the speed restriction would affect progress. With a mere ten coaches in tow, 5,400 bhp would have been more than ample to quickly race up to normal maximum speed, but today the Crewe driver kept 50007/D400 in check with nothing higher than 82mph allowed before passing Tebay. This hampered the attack on the higher slopes of Shap but nevertheless the summit was cleared at an easy 67mph, slightly better than when D400 last passed this way four years earlier. Freewheeling down towards Carlisle with the power controller closed, speed briefly ran up to 92mph but this did little to regain the arrears or placate those looking for a reminder of past glories on the WCML.

Riding with the two '50s' was a pair of fitters; Mike Woodhouse and Chris Lunn from Laira depot.

In fact they had accompanied the locomotives on the run up to London on Friday afternoon and even slept on board overnight at Clapham Junction, prior to the early start on Saturday. At Carlisle before the return working departed, the lads from Laira persuaded Mr Hudson to waive the speed restriction for a short time, thereby allowing the locomotives a final hurrah at their maximum service speed.

Following another photo stop at Penrith, the pair lifted 1Z38 past Shap at 81mph and on the run down the hill speed raced briefly up to 103½mph before the Laira pair glided through Tebay at 101. Gravity assisted it may have been, "storming" it certainly wasn't but the brief dalliance of ton-up running was most fitting, and appreciated by those whose dedication had ensured both locomotives performed faultlessly all day. Continuing onwards from Grayrigg, the smarter pace continued with several miles being covered in the low 90s. This lifted the average speed from Penrith to Preston up to a respectable 75.5mph.

From now on any trains featuring Class 50s would be timed with regard to the maximum speed of 75 mph - resulting in some very long days. The next tour ran on a cloudless Saturday 16 May as the 'Chiltern Atmospheric' organised by the Panshanger Rail Group took D400/50007 from Aylesbury to Plymouth via Greenford, Reading, Castle Cary and Yeovil Pen Mill. Following a two hour break in Plymouth, 50033 replaced 50007 for the return run via Gloucester and Kemble.

The following weekend saw the official Network SouthEast finale of Class 50 operations on the Waterloo to Exeter route. On Sunday 24 May, 50033 was publicised in advance as working a diagram starting at Waterloo while the celebrity pairing of

D400 and 50030 *Repulse* worked the 10.00 Waterloo - Exeter relief service during the NSE 'Network Day' on 5 October 1991, seen here upon arrival at Exeter station. *Derek Riley*

D400 and 50007 was allocated to two return trips between Exeter and Salisbury. The restricted maximum speed of the duo was viewed as good reason to not allow running east of Salisbury. Still permitted to run at 100 mph, 50033 flashed a traction motor on the previous day while working up to London on the 14.22 from Exeter, rendering it unavailable for its Sunday commitments. A controller with a sense of humour however, found 60033 to work in its place as far as Salisbury - its maximum speed of 60mph didn't matter as engineering work resulted in very slow running.

Crowds flocked to the line for the final day's running, rendering the short rake of coaches provided for the busiest trains inadequate. With 50007 and D400 parked in the bay platform at Salisbury before they worked west for the final time, Mr Hudson paid tribute to the staff at Laira depot and the train crews on the Waterloo to Exeter route, praising their

dedication in keeping the Class 50s going for so long.

On the last run, the 1V17 16.55 Waterloo - Exeter, leading locomotive 50007 carried a commemorative headboard proclaiming 'FAREWELL CLASS 50'. For the last empty stock movement from Exeter to Laira Carriage Sidings, the failed 50033 was marshalled into the formation to provide a final triple header (visually at least).

On Saturday 13 June, D400 and 50007 were reunited for an eventful trip from Waterloo to Chester going by the name of the 'Court Chester'. Once again the weather was fantastic, delighting the hoards of photographers, many of whom chased it by car as it took a meandering route to Deeside via the East Midlands and South Yorkshire.

The return journey was routed via Shrewsbury and Wolverhampton, but it was here that the

operational problems so often besetting railtours began to take effect. Overhead line damage saw 1Z36 diverted to Stafford, but instead of making its way south up the WCML to Nuneaton, it was sent back through the West Midlands to Birmingham New Street. By the time Nuneaton was reached via Water Orton, the train was around 90 minutes late and in serious danger of being prevented from getting home due to weekend line possessions for engineering works being taken. Just to make matters worse, the train incurred further delays at Nuneaton awaiting train crew for the Midland Main Line.

On arrival at Bedford just before midnight, BR threw in the towel, declared the train as terminated and un-coupled the '50s' before inviting customers to join the last HST to St Pancras or leave the station and make their own forward transport arrangements. Unsurprisingly this incensed the participants who, having paid for a

50007 *Sir Edward Elgar* leads D400 through Tisbury, whilst hauling the very last run, the 16.55 Waterloo - Exeter on 24 May 1992. 50007 was adorned with a commemorative headboard to mark the end of Class 50 haulage on the route. *Mark Few*

First of the last

tour back to London Waterloo via Bletchley Flyover, Oxford and Twickenham demanded better treatment

With a potential riot brewing, the station staff called in the British Transport Police who after being briefed on the facts sided with the punters and told the staff to put the '50s' back on the train. Eventually the train continued with a final leg to St Pancras, thus enabling 50007/D400 to make a rare visit to the London terminus of the Midland Railway. The arrival time of around 03.00 on Sunday morning, over two and a half hours later than advertised, and long after the London Underground had stopped running meant a not insignificant taxi bill for British Rail and some very late arrivals home.

The rest of 1992 remained quiet on the Class 50 front, but on Sunday 21 June, D400/50007 worked the Waterloo to Andover leg of a steam hauled trip organised by NSE. On the return run, the Class 50s were added to the train at Salisbury and worked

50007/D400 at Salisbury station having worked the penultimate booked Class 50 service, the 15.43 Exeter - Waterloo, on 24 May 1992.

Peter Goodman

back to London in a rare quadruple header with the two steam locomotives tucked inside. An open day at Thornaby Depot on Teeside brought a rare visit to he North East for D400 in September.

The next tour involving D400 didn't take place until early December, when D400/50033 were provided for a trip to north Wales taking in Blaenau Ffestiniog

and Holyhead. Dubbed the 'Festive Fifties', the dismal weather and poor turnout made for a less than festive atmosphere on board - the reduced numbers a sign that interest in the Class 50s could not be guaranteed. The adding of 50033 to the railtour roster helped to break the monotony of D400/50007 working all trains, with a "perm two from three" approach being taken from now on.

D400 and 50007 work 'The Court Chester' through Pinxton on 13 June 1992. **Mark Burrows**

A major factor on the resurrection of 50050 as D400 was the direct involvement of *RAIL* magazine in launching a fundraising appeal for the venture and in the farewell Class 50 programme. From a personal perspective, former *RAIL* Editor **MURRAY BROWN** recounts the exciting times to promote the Class 50s and his involvement in transforming the fortunes of *Fearless*.

The campaign to highlight the plight of the first of the Class 50 fleet and to promote the dwindling '50' fleet began in 1990. To do this, the plan was to have 50050 *Fearless* put back into good order and repainted as it was when it first emerged from Vulcan Foundry in 1967 as D400. To enable this to take place the idea would need the blessing of two organisations - Network SouthEast which operated the Waterloo to Exeter route, the locomotives for which were maintained at Laira, and the Great Western Area Fleet Engineer and his staff who ran Laira depot in Plymouth.

Chris Green was the boss of NSE, who never missed a trick with

publicity, and Geoff Hudson was the Area Fleet Engineer. Whilst Mr Green was more than happy to co-operate, it would, of necessity, fall on Mr Hudson's shoulders to commit to cosseting 50050 *Fearless*. Top marks to Geoff Hudson for entering into the spirit of things

RAIL magazine had introduced news phonelines which offered readers the chance to hear a weekly 'hot off the press' news service covering events, railtours and traction news. It was decided to start an individual Class 50 phoneline - 0898 444050 - solely to give the latest Class 50 news.

Every Friday, I would ring up Laira depot - InterCity Engineer, Roland

Dellar - to ascertain what was in for repair and which were available for use on the Waterloo to Exeter service that weekend. It was a runaway success and amazed everyone at *RAIL* just how successful the phoneline service was. The phoneline raised money and it was this which was earmarked for 50050.

50050 had been stopped at Laira on 17 August 1990. It had suffered a main generator flashover the day before whilst working the 1O32 06.45 Exeter - Waterloo. A replacement generator was ordered and arrived on 29 September, but was used in a different locomotive. 50050's future was looking bleak. After many phone calls between the

Wearing a headboard to mark the involvement of *RAIL* in the revival of 50050 as D400, the locomotive stands alongside a now-withdrawn 50007 *Sir Edward Elgar* at the Laira Open Day on 15 September 1991.
Mark Few

interested parties, the plans emerged for it to be put back into service, sponsored by the readers of *RAIL*.

Besides the phoneline, an appeal was also set up and there was a magnificent response, indicative of the popularity of the scheme and the wish to see the doyen of the class resurrected. Of course, this raised the chance that 50050/D400 would not head to the breaker's yard when finally withdrawn.

A valued contribution from Geoff Hudson was his decision to use overhauled components from the start, rather than used components taken from withdrawn '50s'.

Overhauled power unit IH6944 was earmarked for D400 but it

was delayed by several weeks at Crewe pending rectification of electrical problems. As soon as it was delivered by road to Laira on 1 February 1991, it was lifted straight into D400.

The following weeks saw hectic activity as D400 took shape. Overhauled bogies from Crewe were fitted in early March and many hours were spent on bodywork repairs by the depot painters to obtain a first class result. Amongst these fitters was Mike Woodhouse, a keen Class 50 aficionado who, years later, is still giving his expertise to preserved Class 50 owners.

Following a trial run to Newton Abbot on March 26th, D400 was ready, give or take a few minor items. The big day came on Saturday 6 April when the locomotive was booked to work the 09.45 Plymouth - Waterloo via Southampton and the 17.15 Waterloo - Exeter. This working was chosen specially to allow as many enthusiasts to see and ride behind it as possible. At Waterloo, a cheque for £3,000 was handed over by *RAIL* reader, Geoff Williams from Westbury to Peter Field, the NSE Director who controlled the South West services. Mr Williams' name had been chosen out of a hat containing the names of all the readers who had contributed towards its resurrection. What a day. D400 was alive and well!

The locomotive was in regular use during the ensuing months but on 21 August it suffered a main generator failure. The

RAIL
No. 146
APRIL 17 - 30, 1991 £1.50
D400 IS HERE!
'YOUR' LOCO IS BACK ON THE RAILS
FULL STORY - SEE PAGES 16/17
D400
Extra 24-page ModelRAIL Exhibition special
ModelRAIL 91
EXHIBITION SPECIAL
BEST FOR TRACTION NEWS

armature had gone 'to earth' and was not in warranty. Of interest is that the last Class 50 power unit overhauled by Crewe Works was the one removed from 50050, IH6965, which had caused the locomotive's removal from service the previous year in August 1990. Talks were now taking place to see if two of the class could be retained for enthusiast specials beyond the planned elimination of the class.

The decision was taken to remove D400's power unit and it was replaced by the one from withdrawn 50048 *Dauntless*. At the Laira Open Day on 15 September, Peter Field, NSE Director for South West announced that D400 would be retained for a year after the remaining 'Hoovers' had been withdrawn by the end of that year.

D400 returned to service after valiant efforts by Laira staff for the Network SouthEast 'Network Day' on 5 October when it double-headed an additional 10.00 Waterloo - Exeter and return with 50030.

In mid November 1991, *RAIL*

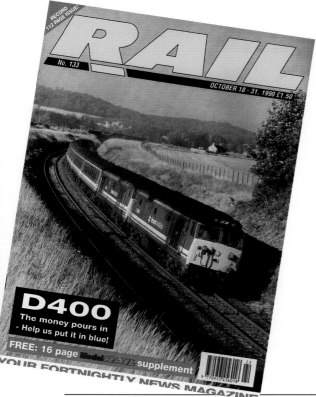

RECORD 112 PAGE ISSUE!
RAIL
No. 133
OCTOBER 18 - 31, 1990 £1.50
D400
The money pours in - Help us put it in blue!
FREE: 16 page total RAIL supplement
YOUR FORTNIGHTLY NEWS MAGAZINE

announced it was to make a bid for D400 when it was withdrawn - expected at the end of 1992. The plan was to procure the locomotive, some spares, and place it with a responsible, proven group.

18 and 19 January 1992 was booked to be the last weekend of Class 50 timetabled use with three machines operational - D400, 50030 and 50033. Meanwhile, a reprieve awaited 50007 *Sir Edward Elgar*. This locomotive had succumbed and was waiting a decision on its future. Were it not for the fact that it was Laira's pet locomotive, 50007 would have joined the queue for towing to a breaker's yard. By mid December, it was inside Laira depot receiving the power unit from popular large-logo machine 50046 *Ajax*. It also received *Ajax*'s bogies.

Poor availability of Class 47/7 replacements meant that the Laira Class 50s continued to be used when circumstances required. To compound matters D400 suffered yet another main generator flashover on 30 January - definitely the Achilles' heel of the class.

Thoughts were now in hand for the farewell specials - the first advertised as the 'Carlisle Fifty Farewell' to be run on Saturday 11 April - a joint promotion with RAIL and NSE. This sold out immediately, so a relief tour, the 'Carlisle Fifty Prelude' was pencilled in for 28 March, although poor bookings saw this one subsequently cancelled. 50030 *Repulse* succumbed with flashover damage on 23 February leaving D400, 50033 *Glorious* and the newly reinstated 50007 as the final three 'Hoovers' on the books. Nominally, *Glorious* was the 'insurance' for the other two railtour machines and 50033 was even repainted by Laira staff!

Hundreds turned out along the route and at Carlisle to see the

The success of the revived D400 and the support of *RAIL* saw Laira depot reinstate 50007 *Sir Edward Elgar* back into traffic for railtour use. Midway through its revival works, 50007 stands in Laira receiving attention alongside D400. *Peter Goodman*

gleaming D400 and 50007 back on home territory on the April 11th tour. A large presentation cheque for £12,000 was handed over by RAIL to John Beer, NSE's West of England Route Manager, towards resurrecting 50007 to working order - the first example of private sponsorship of a locomotive which was still on BR's books.

Geoff Hudson, who was in the cab of D400 on the return journey had sanctioned 100mph down Shap as both locomotives had performed impeccably on the way North. Considering the weeks of problems encountered with both locomotives at Laira, this was another indication of the efforts of the Devon depot and its staff's enthusiasm.

Then it was the final day of celebration on the Waterloo to Exeter route on 24 May - another wish by Mr Hudson to see the locomotives out in style. 50033 disgraced itself when working up to the capital on the Saturday but D400 and 50007 played to the galleries all day.

The Laira staff managed to keep the three celebrities in full running order and they saw extensive railtour duties throughout 1993, their last full year. A reduction in the maximum speed of the locomotives was introduced to try to ensure their longevity.

Of course, Laira's enthusiasm with the 'Hoovers' extended beyond D400. Another example was on 5 February 1994 when 50033 was repainted and de-named as D433

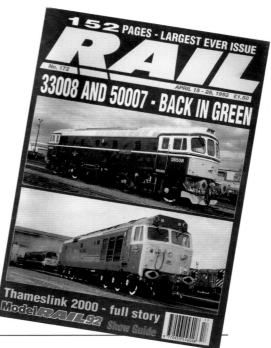

In gloomy conditions, D400 and 50007 *Sir Edward Elgar* head through the Lune Gorge at Dillicar with the returning Carlisle to Waterloo 'Carlisle Fifty Farewell' railtour on 11 April 1992. **Martin Loader**

to be paired with matching D400 on the Class 40 Appeal's 'Midland Scotsman' tour to Glasgow, thus recreating a sight unseen for nearly a quarter of a century. At Glasgow, a cheque was handed over to Geoff Hudson from Ruth Furtek, wife of Paul Furtek of Locomaster Profiles towards the cost of repainting D433 in that guise.

That wasn't the end of Laira's efforts for *Glorious* though. With the news that the NRM was wishing to claim it for the national

Right: Howard Johnston (on the left), the then-publisher of *RAIL* presents a cheque for £12,000 to Geoff Hudson and John Beer at Carlisle during the 'Carlisle Fifty Farewell' tour on 11 April 1992 towards the costs of resurrecting 50007. **Mark Bowerbank**

collection, it was transformed into large logo livery in preparation for the handover, its last outing being a run from York to Scarborough and back on 20 March 1994. The cost of this repaint and that of

D400 into 50050 was paid for by proceeds from railtours and sponsorship by Pathfinder Tours and Locomaster Profiles.

The Class 50 era on the national

The life & times of 50050 *Fearless*

D400 and 50007 *Sir Edward Elgar* pass through Umborn on 24 May 1992, during the last day of Class 50 workings on the Waterloo to Exeter route. **Mark Burrows**

system pre-privatisation finally came to an end on 26 March 1994 with 50050 and 50007 powering the '50 Terminator', its entry into Paddington that evening being a

celebratory raucous affair!

RAIL had inquired if it might be able to buy D400/50050 as a private sale but the NSE hierarchy decreed it should go out to tender. Harry Schneider was the fortunate bidder. 50007 *Sir Edward Elgar* went to the Class 40 Appeal.

The campaign by RAIL was an outstanding success. Not only did it ensure, major disasters such as fire permitting, that D400 would be there at the end and thus enter preservation, but it was enthusiasts calling the phone line to get the latest weekly updates that provided the impetus and funding.

Of course, we should remember that D400 was not the only 'Hoover' to be mollycoddled. 50007 was also brought back from the brink when it could so easily have been carted off like so many

of its classmates. Full credit to Laira staff who took the decision to keep 50033 *Glorious* in working order. So, not only did Network SouthEast and Laira keep to their word by resurrecting D400, they kept it running for a year after its brethren were all finished from regular service - plus they kept two other Class 50s operational into the bargain!

Besides acknowledging the backing by Network SouthEast, the real heroes of this story are the Laira staff, headed by Geoff Hudson and Depot Engineer Malcolm Wishart. What they did in terms of going out of their way to enter into the spirit of the moment, battling against continuing failures and bringing so much pleasure to thousands of enthusiasts had never been seen before, nor equalled since. Gentleman, well done, and consider yourselves truly commended.

First of the last

LOCOMASTER PROFILES AND THE FAREWELL CLASS 50 TOURS

By Paul Furtek

"Locomaster Profile's involvement in the last years of the Class 50s on BR was to provide funding for two things. Part of the proceeds of the CLASS 50 FINALE video went towards the maintenance budget for keeping D400, 50007 and 50033 in traffic. As NSE were not funding the three remaining locomotives, the funds from the video and profits from their railtours is what financially kept them in traffic. Part of the proceeds of THE FALL & RISE video went towards the cost of repainting 50033 into BR blue as D433 for its trip to Glasgow on 5 February 1994. For this tour Laira depot also gave D400 a repaint so that both locomotives would look identically resplendent for the tour to Glasgow. Although this was the plan when Locomaster agreed to fund the cost of 50033's repaint, I still remember Geoff Hudson ringing me approx ten days before the tour was due to run to tell me that because of the depot's heavy HST workload it was not going to be possible to repaint D400. He was apologetic and disappointed - and so was I. So imagine my surprise when I turned up at Laira for the roll out of D433 only to see D400 had been repainted after all. Credit for getting that job done must go to Depot Engineer Malcolm Wishart who took it upon himself to see that Laira did send not one, but two resplendent engines to Glasgow on the 'Midland Scotsman' charter."

In typical Settle & Carlisle weather, with the clouds hanging low over the fells, D433 and D400 cross Smardale Viaduct with the 1Z42 Class 40 Appeal 06:58 Birmingham New Street – Glasgow Central 'Midland Scotsman' railtour on 5 February 1994.

Martin Loader

The life & times of 50050 *Fearless*

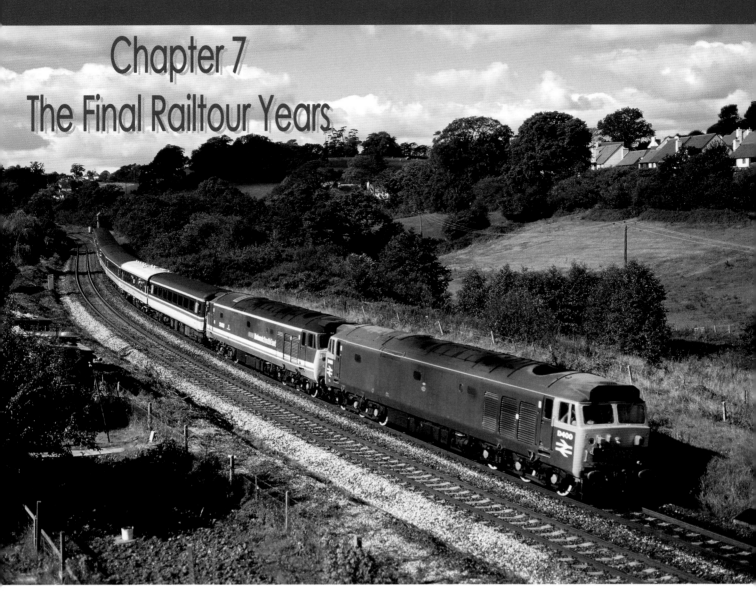

Starting to look a little weather-worn, both D400 and 50033 *Glorious* would soon get attention from Laira's painters. The pair work the 'Atlantic Coast Express' tour from Plymouth to Meldon Quarry on 25 September 1993, seen heading through Totnes. *Mark Burrows*

The first engagement of 1993 produced the regular blue and green machines for another trip with a Welsh theme. Originating at Manchester, the 'Knighton Horse' tour employed a Class 47 as far as Gloucester where the '50s' took over for a run via Cardiff and the Swansea District line, before taking the Central Wales line back up to Knighton. Such was the excitement locally that a civic reception was on hand to greet the train on its arrival. The draw of Class 50s debuting on this route was insufficient to fill the train however, and once again there were many vacant seats on board.

There was a sensible gap of four months to the next trip, during which anyone previously overdosing on Class 50 railtours could dry out. Running on Bank Holiday Monday 31 May, the use of Class 37s on the first section from Crewe to Exeter helped to attract additional bookings. This was the first time that all three retained Class 50s were used on the same tour, and with all the mileage being on 'home turf' in the west, patronage was much greater. D400/50033 relieved the Class 37s at Exeter and worked as far as Plymouth, where 50007 took over for a solo run to Penzance and back. Then all three Class 50s worked together in multiple up to Bristol Temple Meads, where the Class 37s reappeared for the run back to Crewe.

One week later the three '50s' worked through to York from Bishops Lydeard on the West Somerset Railway, with a trip originating from Minehead behind steam traction. Triple heading was necessary as on arrival at York, the green machine 50007 would be dropped off to spend a couple of months on display at the National Railway Museum (NRM). A single Class 50 could not be trusted to work back from York on its own, so in order to ensure the return leg was double-headed, the outward run featured 8,100 bhp of English Electric muscle at the helm. 50007 remained at York until August Bank Holiday weekend, when it worked back to the Western on the return leg of another tour, double-heading with the green liveried 47833.

With 50007 on holiday in Yorkshire, a July trip from London Waterloo to Exeter, Barnstaple and Exmouth was bound to produce D400/50033. After double-heading to Exeter, the Class 50s were marshalled in top and tail formation for the branch line sections but on the return from Exmouth, 50033 derailed while descending from Exeter Central to Exeter St David's station. This resulted in D400 working back to Waterloo on its own.

Late summer and autumn trips were much simpler affairs than all day railtouring, and well patronised by enthusiasts as the final end for the Class 50s, expected to be at the end of March 1994 edged nearer.

On Sunday 19 September, D400 and the repatriated 50007 were

NSE 50033 and D400 are paired together on 4 April 1992, providing a colourful contrast. *Ian Horner*

turned out to work the 1Z50 08.25 Plymouth - Newport in connection with a BR gala event taking place at Newport station. The following weekend again saw use for all three Class 50s

beginning on Saturday 25 September when D400/50033 worked another BR organised trip, the 'Atlantic Coast Express' from Plymouth to Meldon Quarry and back. The rolling stock was

D400 works a demonstration freight train along the Paignton and Dartmouth Railway on 16 October 1993, passing Britannia. This event saw the Laira trio join preserved 50002 and 50042 at the heritage line.
Mark Burrows

unusually formed of air conditioned Mk 2 coaches, and worked down from Paddington as a relief service via Bristol by 47484 *Isambard Kingdom Brunel*. On the Sunday, 50007/033 worked a simple return trip from Plymouth to Penzance.

The final outing for D400 in 1993 took place on Saturday 16 October, when it worked a 1Z50 17.10 Paignton - Paddington with 50033. This was in connection with a Class 50 themed event on the Paignton and Dartmouth Steam Railway, when the BR trio joined preserved 50002 and 50042 on the heritage line. The outward trip from Paddington had been worked by 50007/033, but squad rotation ensured everyone had the chance to sample all three

remaining Class 50s on the main line also.

April 1994 marked a major political reorganisation of Britain's railway with the creation of Railtrack and the Train Operating Units ahead of the franchising process due to start soon after. Less significant in the grand scheme of things was the final withdrawal of the remaining Class 50 locomotives, planned for the end of the financial year. This made the remaining trips, planned for the first quarter of 1994 potentially the final outings on the main line.

On Saturday 8 January, the first tour of the year featured yet another track bash around Wales as D400/50007 were provided for

the 1Z16 06.25 from Crewe routed via Stafford, Selly Oak, Gloucester, Cardiff and the Swansea District line to Clarbeston Road. From there 60065 was added to the rear in order to take in Robeston and Waterston oil terminals, running in top and tail formation. The return run was routed via Cockett. On Sunday afternoon while travelling back to Laira depot, the pair of Class 50s was commandeered at Exeter to assist an ailing HST over the Devon banks to Plymouth.

The final railtours featured regular repaints as great efforts were made to ensure the Class 50's were sent off in style. On Saturday 5 February the 'Midland Scotsman' was advertised as returning Class

Mark Burrows

First of the last

50007 and D400 make a rare appearance beneath the trainshed at St Pancras, with an early hours arrival at the London terminus, just after 03.00 on Sunday 14 June 1992. The very-late running 'Court Chester' railtour - which the pair had hauled - had been dogged with problems on the return section of the trip. **Peter Goodman**

50s to Shap, Beattock and Glasgow Central for the final time. To ensure the event passed off properly, the video company Locomaster Profiles sponsored the repainting of 50033 into BR blue livery with original running number D433. To ensure its partner on the day also looked its best, Laira depot repainted D400 - this time finished off with correctly sized numbers. A 1970s style headboard adorned lead locomotive D433 as the 1Z42 06.58 Birmingham - Glasgow Central headed for Scotland via the Settle and Carlisle line. After pausing at Appleby station the train was reversed a few hundred yards to enable a 'run past' to be staged - giving the passengers a better chance to photograph the superbly turned out locomotives.

These were the first Class 50s to work into Glasgow since 1988 and the first in original livery since the last of the class was transferred to the Western Region in 1976. The 17.03 return run from Glasgow

Central was routed straight back to the West Midlands via the WCML. Two weeks later 50033 had its TOPS numbers and nameplates restored for another trip from Paddington with 50007.

The penultimate weekend of action began on Friday 18 March when the 1Z50 21.15 York - Newquay 'Cornish Caper' set off

behind a Class 47. At Bristol Temple Meads, the immaculate pairing of 50007 in green livery and 50050 - restored to large logo livery for the first time in seven years and reunited with its *Fearless* nameplates and crests - took over.

At Plymouth, 50033 also just repainted into large logo livery was added to the rear in order to

50007 *Sir Edward Elgar* and D400 pause at Edale station for a photo stop during the Court Chester tour on 13 June 1992.   **Peter Goodman**

Vintage traction galore on show as D400 and D433 overtake a Strathclyde PTE liveried Class 101 DMU on the approach to Glasgow with the Class 40 Appeal's 'Midland Scotsman' tour on 5 February 1994. For this tour Locomaster Profiles sponsored the repaint of 50033 into D433 and Laira joined in with the spirit by refreshing D400's paintwork to give a gleaming pair of Class 50s for the tour. *Hans Chowdhury*

work the Newquay and St Ives branches in top and tail formation. After a break at Penzance, the two large logo machines; 50033/050 worked the 1Z50 13.10 Penzance - York throughout. The following day 50033 took its final trains, a return trip to Scarborough before transferring to the custodianship of the NRM. This left 50050 to work back to Laira depot solo, via a break en-route at Saltley.

On Tuesday 22 March, 50050 resumed its trip back to Devon and happened to be the nearest locomotive to hand when a Class 47 hauling the 1V46 09.18 Manchester - Plymouth failed near Abbotswood Junction. *Fearless* was called upon to assist the train on to Bristol Temple Meads where it was terminated, going down in history as the final normal service train hauled by a Class 50 on the nationalised British Rail network.

On Saturday 26 March, the curtain came down on the chequered

career of the Class 50 with the running of the '50 Terminator' from Waterloo to Penzance and back to Paddington. The two remaining locomotives 50007/050 were provided and with 50050 in the lead, worked the 1Z40 08.52

from Waterloo with a set of Inter-City liveried air conditioned coaches in tow.

After running round at Exeter St David's the train continued onwards as 1Z07 but problems

50033 *Glorious* and D400 haul a special through the attractive surroundings of Cockwood Harbour on 16 October 1993, with a special returning from the Paignton and Dartmouth Railway, where they had appeared for a Class 50 themed special event. *Anton Kendall*

occurred when 50050's engine shut down shortly after leaving Newton Abbot. This was traced to a fault with the stock and after being restarted at Plymouth, no further problems were encountered with either '50'. After a break of just over an hour at Penzance, the final Class 50 hauled train operated by British Rail set sail, running as the 1Z50 17.35 Penzance - Paddington.

Both locomotives remained restricted to 75mph - this was not lifted for the final train, which was a pity as with limited stops and 100mph stock, a fast run would have made for a fitting finale. On the night, delays outside Reading and a slow run into Paddington preceded the 'Terminator' terminating at Paddington some 22 minutes late at 23.38. Amidst a fanfare of horn blowing the train came to a stand at platform 10 and another chapter of British railway history was closed.

After a busy and varied career lasting nearly 27 years, 50050 returned with 50007 back to Laira depot after the tour to await its fate. What would the future hold for the pioneer Class 50 now?

Above: A repainted 50050 *Fearless* double-heads with 50007 *Sir Edward Elgar*, whilst hauling the Cornish Caper railtour on 19 March 1994.

Craig Munday

Below: D400 and 50007 pause at a rather gloomy Haverfordwest with the 'Dyfed Dub-Dub' railtour on 8 January 1994. *Peter Goodman*

... 5 February 1994 ...

First of the last

The second railtour to operate in 1994 was organised by the Class 40 Appeal, who went on to be custodians of 50007 *Sir Edward Elgar* later that year when it was purchased by some members of the group. For the 'Midland Scotsman' tour on 5 February 1994, 50033 was returned to retro-1970 style as D433, joining D400 which was given a quick spruce up to give an immaculate matching pair of BR blue Class 50s.

Opposite Page Upper: Work completed, D433 and D400 stand inside the shed at Laira following repainting,. *Paul Furtek*

Opposite Page Lower: The repainted pair line up next to each other at Laira on 2 February 1994., *Brian Morrison*

Inset Middle: A symmetrical study of the cabs of D433 and D400. *Paul Furtek*

Above Centre: A piper greets the arrival of D433 and D400 to Glasgow Central after a successful outward journey on the 'Midland Scotsman' tour. *Scott Ryder*

Above: Following repainting into BR blue D400 and D433 head a test train of TPO coaches through Rewe on 2 February 1994. *Anton Kendall*

Middle Left: D433 and D400 stand at Carlisle station with the 'Midland Scotsman' tour. In the early years of the locomotives they would have frequently called at Carlisle whilst on WCML services. *Ian Horner*

Left: Wearing a suitable headboard, D433 and D400 pause at Appleby. *Ian Horner*

The life & times of 50050 *Fearless*

As the penultimate BR tour approached, it was time to say goodbye once more to D400 and welcome back 50050 *Fearless*, as both 50033 and 50050 were repainted into BR large logo colours. Special care was taken with 50033 which was destined to be delivered to the National Railway Museum during the tour and its bodysides were covered in brown paper to protect the paint finish on the locomotive. The above three photos show the work underway at Laira.

All: Peter Goodman

Above Right: 50050 and 50007 head the 'Cornish Caper' at Carbis Bay station with 50033 on the back of the formation. **Hans Chowdhury**

Right: 50050 stands ready to run from York to Saltley depot, having said farewell to 50033.

Greg Edwards

First of the last

Above: The penultimate railtour was Pathfinders Tours 'Cornish Caper', which used the surviving trio of 50007, 50033 and 50050. 50050 and 50007 stand at Plymouth on the morning of 19 March 1994 - the first time that 50050 had worked a train in large logo blue livery since July 1987.
Mark Burrows

Inset: Laira Fitter Chris Reece refits the *Fearless* nameplates and crests a couple of days before the tour. This was the first time that 50050 had carried *Fearless* nameplates since its repaint as 50400 in 1991. *Paul Furtek*

Right: 50033 *Glorious* and 50050 *Fearless* pass Buckstead whilst working the Cornish Caper tour.
Martin Loader

... Cornish Caper ...

The life & times of 50050 *Fearless*

1967 ... The End ... 1994
Riding the 50 Terminator

Having been involved in filming the Class 50 rundown through his company, Locomaster Profiles, **PAUL FURTEK** was given a unique chance to film the historic farewell tour live from the footplate.

First of the last

The Class 50 was the last class of locomotive to be withdrawn from service by British Rail. Like other classes before them, the final survivors were given a fitting send off with a series of farewell railtours. In the case of the '50s', three locomotives - 50007 *Sir Edward Elgar*, 50033 *Glorious* and D400/50050 *Fearless* remained in traffic with Network SouthEast for use on charter trains. The class had ceased working regular passenger trains on the Waterloo to Exeter route during the early months of 1992.

The last three operational '50s' were based at Laira depot in Plymouth - in the care of Area Fleet Manager, Geoff Hudson. I had worked closely with Geoff for several years, producing two video documentaries detailing the final years of the '50s', with particular emphasis on how the fleet was managed and maintained. Geoff was aware that the 'Deltics' had received the best send-off of any modern traction class under BR, and he was determined to ensure that the '50s' bowed out in similar style. And so it was, in their final

Left: After reversing at Exeter St. Davids, the Pathfinder Tours '50 Terminator' railtour is seen here passing through Totnes, hauled by 50007 *Sir Edward Elgar* & 50050 *Fearless*, running as the 1Z07 13.17 Exeter St. Davids to Penzance on 26 March 1994. *John Chalcroft / www.railphotoprints.co.uk*

years of traffic, the last three Laira-based locomotives underwent various repaints and identity transformations, as the trio travelled far and wide on a variety of charter trains.

The final railtour for the class was to be the '50 Terminator' - promoted by Pathfinder Tours and scheduled for Saturday 26 March 1994. The train would appropriately cover the key routes the Class 50s had worked over since the fleet completed its transfer from the LMR in 1976 - London Waterloo to Exeter, Exeter to Penzance and Penzance to London Paddington.

The weekend before the final trip, Pathfinder organised another tour, the 'Cornish Caper' - from Bristol to Penzance, Newquay and St Ives. Afterwards, I received a phone call from Geoff who told me how he had been sitting in the leading cab of 50050 (the rear locomotive of a pair), listening to the front locomotive (50007) pounding its way up the steeply-graded Luxulyan Valley - and how impressive the sound was. He suggested we should somehow try to capture the 'live' sound of a '50' on the main line for posterity, while filming from the cab on the final tour in a week's time.

This sounded like a great idea, but it was something I had never previously attempted, and I wondered about the logistics of such an operation, and whether the results would actually do it justice. The main drawback was that the driving cabs were so well sound-proofed, that little of the engine itself could be heard from the leading cab. Geoff and I agreed that the sound would have to be picked up through an open window in the rear cab, while the pictures were recorded at the front. The problem with this scenario was how to connect the microphone to the camera? The solution was to obtain a long lead - a very

long lead, and hope that it worked.

We realised there was no time for a dry run, because there was only one Class 50-hauled train left on which to try it - the upcoming weekend's farewell railtour. Just to add to the pressure, there was less than a week left to organise it all - but taking everything into account, we both decided it was worth giving it a go.

While Geoff took care of the admin' issues - paperwork, passes and traction inspectors to enable me to travel in the driving cabs, I set about gathering the recording equipment together for the trip. This included obtaining a purpose-made (80 feet long) microphone cable that would run between the locomotive cabs. As soon as I collected it - on the Thursday before the tour, the cable was hastily couriered down to Laira depot where it arrived with one day to spare - phew! Depot Engineer Malcolm Wishart arranged for the long blue lead to be fitted into 50050, but unfortunately there just wasn't time for me to go down to Plymouth to carry out an 'in situ' test. I would therefore have to wait until the day of the tour itself to see if it actually worked, and in particular whether the custom made shielded lead would resist the interference from the locomotives' numerous electrical components.

In what seemed like the blink of an eye, the big day was upon us and I was up at the crack of dawn on the Saturday morning, ready to make my way across London to Clapham Junction where the two locomotives; 50007 and 50050 had been stabled overnight. There I met Laira's riding inspectors who would chaperone the '50s' for the duration of the day's tour - Geoff Hudson, Malcolm Wishart, fitter Mike Woodhouse and electrician Richard (Dickie) Daw. They all

End of an era. 50050 *Fearless* and 50007 *Sir Edward Elgar* stand at the blocks upon arrival at Paddington with the '50 Terminator' farewell railtour. Although both locomotives would be withdrawn a few days later, happily both were bought for preservation.

Nick Green

waited with baited breath while I set up the filming equipment.

With the microphone connected to the sound lead in the rear cab, I plugged the other end into the camera... switched it on... plugged in the headphones... and, hey presto! - there was the voice of Mike Woodhouse from the other end saying *"testing, testing"*. A smiling Geoff remarked *"there you go - wired for sound!"* Little did he or I realise at the time, that this would be the start of a whole series of video programmes.

So with relieved smiles all round, we settled down for the short light engine run to Waterloo where the two '50s' were attached to the train. The sun was shining, the station was heaving and the '50 Terminator' was a sell-out. It had all the makings of a great, if somewhat sad, day.

With the large logo liveried 50050 in the lead, train 1Z40 set off from Waterloo 'right time' at 08.52 on the first leg of the journey to Exeter. As driver Tony Kowalski opened the power handle to notch seven for the first time, the sound of the locomotives at full chat in the headphones could be heard loud and clear. And I do mean loud! Mike and Dickie were stationed in 50050's rear cab working as sound engineers,

enthusiastically opening and closing the windows while using a windshield which Mike had hastily made from his technical notes.

A spirited run through the London suburbs saw us arrive a few minutes early at Woking, where we were duly checked by signals just outside the station. There then followed a virtual 'full on' standing start, with more spectacular audio results secured via the microphone in the rear cab. As we progressed, there was barely a bridge or station without a posse of photographers waiting to capture the passing of the very last Class 50-hauled train on BR. With the added bonus of

First of the last

The end is near as 50050 and 50007 stand at London Waterloo, having arrived light engine from Clapham Junction, where they had been stabled the previous evening.

Rob Sandford

wall-to-wall sunshine, this would set the pattern for the entire outward journey to Penzance.

The first scheduled stop was at Basingstoke, where we were greeted by an army of photographers. Following another spirited departure, we were soon passing Worting Junction where the train diverged under Battledown Flyover to take the Salisbury route. Thanks to some more excellent running, arrival at a packed Salisbury station was two minutes early. Here we had the first crew change of the day, with driver Bernie Shergold taking over for the remainder of the run to Exeter. Bernie entered into the spirit of the occasion by sounding the horn at just about every photographer we saw - all of whom were out to capture the sight of the train on a route which they had regularly worked on since 1980.

We were soon on the single track section from Wilton Junction to Templecombe, including an impressive run up to the summit at Buckhorn Weston tunnel. Our arrival at Yeovil Junction was two minutes early, where the tour was booked to stand for 25 minutes. The two Class 50s posed in the spring sunshine alongside 'Dutch' liveried 37012, which was stabled on an engineering train. The '50s' set off again on time at 11.25 after which came the highlight of the run over 'The Mule' - as the Waterloo to Exeter route was known by many Class 50 enthusiasts. As we were again running slightly early, Driver Shergold put the train brakes in on the approach to Seaton Junction

Exeter Driver John Morton is seen at the controls of 50007 while working the outward leg of the tour between Exeter and Plymouth.

Paul Furtek

The '50 Terminator' ran from Waterloo to Exeter via the old Southern Railway route, and then after reversal at Exeter St. Davids carried on to Penzance via the former Great Western mainline, thus covering both routes that were home to the class in their latter years. 50050 *Fearless* & 50007 *Sir Edward Elgar* are pictured rounding the curve at Oborne, near Sherborne, running as 1Z40 08.52 Waterloo - Exeter. **Martin Loader**

station, before letting speed trickle down to 20mph. He then gave 50050/007 the lot for a full-on blast through the remains of the derelict station as the '50s' began the assault on the six mile 1-in-80 climb to Honiton tunnel. It was stirring stuff.

With the fireworks over (for now), we were briefly held in Honiton loop to cross a Waterloo-bound Class 159 DMU. Progress was then slow (but on time) to Exmouth Junction, where we were held again to allow a local stopping service to come off the Exmouth branch. After the big drop from Exeter Central, arrival at St David's was nine minutes late at 12.28. Here there was a break of nearly one hour for the

passengers while the train proceeded to Riverside Yard, where the locomotives ran round before continuing westwards to Penzance.

Mike and I now had a race against time to remove the sound lead from 50050 and re-install it into 50007 - which would be the leading locomotive from Exeter. There was the transfer of all the filming equipment onto the green machine to take care of too. With the job successfully done, we were soon heading back into St David's station, to pick up the tour participants once again. Restarting with Exeter driver John Morton at the controls, and now running as the 1Z07 13.17 Exeter - Penzance, the '50 Terminator'

headed for the scenic south Devon coastline.

Soon afterwards, we faced the first drama of the day. Having been brought to a stand at a signal near the disused Exminster signalbox, we were informed that there was a failed HST in front of us. The Laira team quickly bailed out and started to walk up the track to offer assistance if required. Fortunately, the stricken HST was soon on the move again but its delay meant that we were now 20 minutes late at Dawlish Warren, where we stopped to pick up Mike and Dickie.

Not surprisingly the scenic sea wall sections at Dawlish and

First of the last

The scene at Exeter St Davids as seen from the footplate of 50007 as photographers record the passing of the last Class 50-hauled train on British Rail. **Paul Furtek**

Teignmouth had attracted plenty of lineside photographers. After running along the Teign estuary, we were soon passing the Aller divergence at the foot of the climb up to Dainton Tunnel. Cue drama number two...

About one third of the way up the bank, Driver Morton noticed that despite the locomotives being at full power, train speed was falling rapidly. He commented that it was as if only one Class 50 was hauling the train - rather than a pair. It later transpired that this was exactly what we had, as 50050 behind us had shut down. Contrary to what many on the tour thought at the time, this was not deliberate. That said, it was an unexpected bonus to hear 50007 (with a dead Class 50 and ten coaches in tow) pounding its way up to the tunnel in spectacular style, eventually passing the summit at 18mph.

It was more of the same after Totnes as *Sir Edward* single-handedly got to grips with Rattery bank, before entering Marley Tunnel just past the top at 30mph. During the climb of Rattery, Mike, in the leading cab of 50050, managed to attract the attention of Driver Morton. He confirmed that *Fearless* wasn't powering - not that there was anything that could be done about it while the train was still on the move. Thanks to the HST failure, we arrived at Plymouth some 20 minutes late. The shutting down of 50050 (which was due to an electrical defect on one of the coaches) meant that we were unable to recover some of the already lost time. This did not actually add further delay to the train - except at Plymouth station, where the fault was found before 50050 was restarted. With both locomotives running normally again, driver Mike Galvin took over the driving duties for the remainder of the outward run to Penzance. Departure from Plymouth was 26 minutes late at 14.45.

After carefully crossing the Royal Albert Bridge at Saltash, the two '50s' were soon back in their stride on the long haul up to Doublebois, the downhill run to Lostwithiel and the subsequent climb to Treverrin tunnel. As luck would have it, we were due to have a ten minute pathing stop at Burngullow Junction prior to entering the-then single-line section to Probus. With a clear signal ahead however, there was no need to stop and suddenly we were running 'right time' again.

A 45 minute break at Penzance during the tour gave the opportunity for a photo-stop. This was the scene at a station that had regularly hosted Class 50s throughout their time on the Western Region. **Richard Smith**

The man who made such an impact on the Class 50 fleet in their twilight years. With his two Class 50s having successfully reached Penzance, a smiling Plymouth Area Fleet Manager Geoff Hudson stands alongside 50007 *Sir Edward Elgar* at Long Rock depot. *Paul Furtek*

Truro marked another stiff test for the locomotives with the start of the nine mile slog up to Scorrier, but the two '50s' mastered the Cornish gradients with relative ease. Thanks to some fine driving from Mike Galvin, we arrived at St Erth 12 minutes early where we held to follow a DMU off the St Ives branch. Our arrival at Penzance was nevertheless two minutes ahead of schedule - and the sun was still shining! The locomotives and rolling stock retired to Long Rock depot for a quick check-over, while Mike and I set about the task of transferring the

sound lead from 50007 back to 50050.

After a break of one hour, the return leg of the tour (1Z50 17.35 Penzance - Paddington) set off from the Cornish terminus four minutes late, with *Fearless* at the sharp end. There was a sense of sadness on the footplate, as everyone realised that the end of the Class 50s was just six hours away. There was also the knowledge that it wasn't just the Class 50s that were coming to an end, because just a few days later, the new age of railway privatisation would begin, thus bringing to an

end the 46 year era of British Rail.

Sadness aside, there was still plenty to enjoy as the farewell tour headed back towards London. With Driver Galvin still at the helm, the gradients to Redruth, Grampound Road and Burngullow provided excellent entertainment, but the most memorable part of the return journey through Cornwall was the climb up Largin Bank from Bodmin Parkway. Rather than take a run up, power was shut off after the station until speed had dropped down to 20mph. Driver Galvin then opened both locomotives up for a rousing assault on Largin. For many years a familiar sound in this part of the world, here for the last time was the distinctive sound of two '50s' at full chat, echoing through the trees in the surrounding Fowey valley.

Having re-traced our steps back into Devon, we rolled into Plymouth on time at 19.16. By now it was dark, and I had been on my feet and looking through the eyepiece of a video camera for the best part of 12 hours or so. Not surprisingly, I fancied resting not only my feet, but also my eyes. Geoff (who had been standing as long as I had), suggested we go and sit in the vacant leading cab of 50007. We had the cab windows open as the '50s' tackled Hemerdon Bank for the last time. It had been a long day and we sat in silence just listening to the magical sound of the locomotives as they did battle with the 1-in-42 gradient. I don't remember much after the rousing run up to Dainton Summit, apart from another stop at Exeter where

Opposite: 50050 *Fearless* and 50007 *Sir Edward Elgar* bow out of BR service in style, whilst working the farewell railtour. The pair are pictured at Yeovil Junction, which in recent years has been the home base for 50050. *Peter Goodman*

First of the last

Driver Galvin finished his turn of duty. From here, Andy Snowden took over the controls for the remainder of the journey to London.

The tour continued via the Berks and Hants route to Reading where after a delay outside the station, the train made its final stop. Here Geoff and I rejoined the others up in the front cab of *Fearless* for the remaining 36 miles to Paddington. It was a spirited run by the '50s' along the Thames Valley, and it was a particularly sad moment for me - passing through my home station at Langley for the very last time on a Class 50. Our good running was interrupted by another signal check near Old Oak Common depot before we made the final approach to Paddington station.

It wasn't until now that there had been any talk on the footplate of the arrival at Paddington, but we all knew there would be a large crowd waiting to greet the very last '50s' to arrive at this long-standing haunt for the class. 50050/007 duly arrived at the terminus some 22 minutes late at 23.38 - marking the end of their 305 mile journey with a poignant fanfare of horns from both locomotives. As the train slowly made its way down the platform, a cordon of photographers could clearly be seen by the buffer stops, waiting to capture another piece of railway history.

No sooner had we reached the stop-blocks then both engines were shut down. There was an eerie silence in the cab as we watched hundreds of people surround the locomotives, jostling

to get their final pictures of a memorable trip.

The empty stock was eventually hauled away to Old Oak Common allowing the '50s' to leave for a light engine run to Reading. As they left Paddington station for the last time with their horns still blaring, it reminded me of when I had been at King's Cross station some 12 years earlier, to witness the 'Deltic' farewell.

As I write this, more than 15 years on from riding the '50 Terminator' on board the locomotives, I feel privileged to have witnessed such an historic and well executed event at such close quarters. This was not just any event, but an event that went down in railway history.

The life & times of 50050 *Fearless*

50050 *Fearless* and 50007 *Sir Edward Elgar* on the single line section at Coker Wood with the farewell railtour on 26 March 1994.

John Chalcroft / www.railphotoprints.co.uk

At 8.50AM on the Saturday 26th March 1994, 50007 *Sir Edward Elgar* and 50050 *Fearless* set off from London Waterloo with the last Class 50-hauled train on BR - 'The 50 Terminator'. With 600 people on board and hundreds more at the lineside, the train ran a 600-mile journey over some long-standing haunts of the class. This DVD, which has been re-issued to mark the trains' 15th anniversary, is a cab ride of that historic journey. To faithfully capture the once-familiar sound of a Class 50 hard at work, both locos were specially **Wired for Sound** to capture 5,400 horsepower of 16CSVT power.

Plymouth's former Area Fleet Manager Geoff Hudson recalls a memorable and occasion in a programme which features challenging gradients, serious thrash, fine scenery and plenty of sunshine and perfectly captures the day's historic events. And you can see and hear it all from the best seat on the train!

The material in this DVD has been digitally re-mastered and includes nearly an hour of additional footage not featured in the original VHS version.

Programme running time approximately 110 minutes

Locomaster Profiles gratefully acknowledge the assistance of Geoff Hudson, Malcolm Wishart, Mike Woodhouse and Dickie Daw and of the drivers and traction inspectors from Salisbury, Exeter and Plymouth in the making of this programme. Without their efforts, this programme would not have been possible.

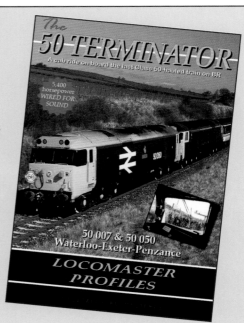

FREEPOST (SL2253), LANGLEY, SLOUGH, SL3 6BP.
www.locomaster.co.uk

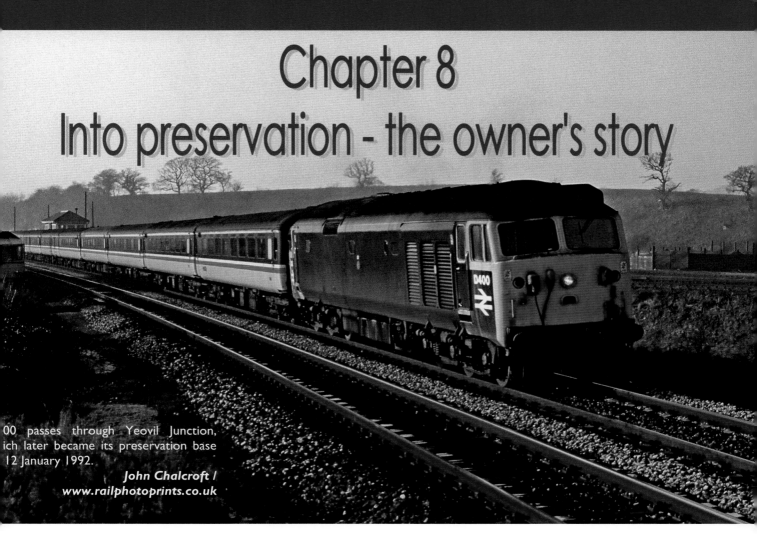

00 passes through Yeovil Junction,
ich later became its preservation base
12 January 1992.

John Chalcroft /
www.railphotoprints.co.uk

Many people dream about owning their own locomotive, but few have actually done it, and even fewer who live and work in another country. 50050 was bought from British Rail in 1994 by Dutch railwayman and enthusiast Harry Schneider. **RICHARD THOMPSON** spoke to him about how he came to buy 50050 and some of the highs and lows since.

Harry Schneider is a railway enthusiast who has held an appreciation for Class 50s since the first time he saw one in 1977, when he caught a train from London Paddington on his way to view the steam locomotive scrapyard at Barry, in South Wales.

Born in 1960, Harry is a career railwayman in his native Netherlands, having started as a driver, before being promoted to Traction Inspector and later a health and safety manager for three years. He still works on the railway to this day, although now as a training centre teacher, where he is responsible for the training and inspection of train drivers. He is licensed to drive trains in The Netherlands and also in Germany.

Harry has always had a keen interest in railway heritage and preservation, both in The Netherlands and also the UK. In 1974 he had his first experience of railway preservation helping to restore steam locomotives - something he would continue to work on for the next 12 years. His love of British traction and railway preservation saw him spending time in the UK working as a volunteer at the Nene Valley Railway in Cambridgeshire and at the now-closed Steamtown railway centre in Carnforth.

Although essentially a steam enthusiast, there was something that Harry found fascinating about Class 50s when he first saw them, as he explains: "The first '50s' I saw were 50011 and 50046 at Paddington station. They were so dirty and noisy, that they were rather reminiscent of steam locomotives, as I have always felt steam locomotives have their own character and the two '50s' I saw that day had character too. It felt like they had personalities of their own."

He remembers being particularly taken with the power of the '50s': "The impressive thing to me was seeing them standing at the buffer stops. It was like a huge explosion - 16 explosions all at once. After that, I went two or three times a year to see these impressive machines in action. I also thought the same of the 'Deltics', which I am also fond of. 'Deltics' and '50s' are what got me interested and involved in modern traction."

What many British enthusiasts probably don't know is Harry Schneider was instrumental in the preservation of British-built

Above: Upon their retirement from BR service in 1994, Harry Schneider placed bids for both 50050 and 50007 *Sir Edward Elgar*, before he learnt that he had successfully purchased 50050. The pair stand at Edale during a stopover on the 'Court Chester' tour on 13 June 1992. *Peter Goodman*

former Woodhead route 'EM2' 1501 when it was withdrawn from use in The Netherlands in 1986, and he has been chairman of the owning group ever since. Was it due to his interest in Class 50s and 'Deltics' which led to the 'EM2s' preservation? "That's a good question. I would have tried to save 1501 anyway, but it was special to me because I was interested in British locomotives and the 'EM2' was a piece of English railway history in The Netherlands. When I was driving it, I realised I was on a British locomotive which was built for use between Sheffield and Manchester."

As an enthusiastic follower of the '50s', Harry had set his heart on buying a Class 50 when the opportunity arose. However, 50050 wasn't his first choice: "It was pure chance I bought 50050. Previously, I had submitted bids for various other Class 50s, including 50027 *Lion*, 50030 *Repulse* and 50007 *Sir Edward Elgar*.

The first Class 50 I attempted to buy was 50027."

With his Class 50 ownership goal clearly set, Harry made a trip to CF Booth's scrapyard in Rotherham, to examine the heavily-stripped Class 50s which had been delivered to the yard in early 1992 for scrapping, but he decided he wouldn't bid for any of them, in view of their poor condition. During his visit to CF Booth's he met Mike Fuller, the owner of 50027, who was in the process of buying 50026 from the scrapyard as a source of spares for his locomotive. In recent years, the owners and support groups of both 50027 and 50050 have worked alongside each other for the benefit of their respective locomotives.

With the Rotherham '50s' discounted, Harry continued his search, examining other '50s' which were put up for disposal by BR: "I went to view 50037 *Illustrious* and 50046 *Ajax*, which

had been included on a tender list that I had been sent. In the case of 50037 and 50046, they were both being stripped of many components and really weren't worth buying, so I decided to wait until the final three were made available. When the final tender was released I put bids in for 50030, then 50050 and 50007." After a tense few weeks waiting to hear if he had been successful, Harry received a phone call to tell him that his bid for 50050 had been accepted.

After several failed bids for other '50s', Harry had managed to buy the pioneer Class 50, but did he realise the significance of his new purchase at the time?: "I was surprised when the EM2 Society wanted to preserve 27000, as it certainly wasn't the best of the surviving 'EM2s', but that's when I realised the British have a love for pioneer locomotives. To me, the fact it was a pioneer wasn't important. Any Class 50 would have been fine for me. I liked all the '50s' and would have been just as happy with 50007 or 50030, both of which I had attempted to buy on that final tender list."

Having bought the locomotive, Harry now had the small matter of finding a home for his new purchase, whilst he considered his plans for its future. Contact was made with John White - the owner of St Leonard's depot - to see if he would allow 50050 to be accommodated at the depot. Thankfully, he agreed to help and Harry states that had he not been able to help with the storage of 50050, he may have been forced to cancel his purchase of the locomotive.

One of Harry's initial plans for 50050 was to export it to The Netherlands for use on railtours: "I wanted to take it to The Netherlands, so that I had my own piece of BR at home. By taking 50050 to The Netherlands, I wanted to impress the Dutch railway enthusiasts with a classic British diesel locomotive design."

It quickly became apparent however, that exporting 50050 to The Netherlands would be extremely expensive and registering it for use there would have been far from straightforward, with Harry stating the registration process was too complicated: "I started investigating running it in The Netherlands and I was saving money at the time to export it, but I didn't necessarily intend it to run on the main line there, and I thought running 50050 on a preserved line would be enough."

With his plans to move 50050 to The Netherlands proving to be more complicated than he had originally thought, it was a chance meeting at the Crewe Open Day in May 1997 with Michael Timms from Deltic 9000 Locomotive Ltd (DNLL), that finally decided the fate of *Fearless*.

DNLL made history in 1996 when the company returned Class 55 'Deltic' D9000 *Royal Scots Grey* to mainline use and it later achieved success in operating the 'Deltic' both on railtours and also for spot-hire use. Negotiations for various other contracts and a number of speculative enquiries convinced DNLL it needed additional traction. As such, DNLL began the restoration of their second locomotive - D9016 *Gordon Highlander* - back to main line use. The company also reached agreement with the National Railway Museum to overhaul 55002 *The King's Own Yorkshire Light Infantry*.

In addition to the planned 'Deltics', DNLL sought other types of traction for mainline use, with the powerful Class 50s becoming its preferred option for a second traction type, although it continued to look at other types to add to its pool of locomotives for use on spot-hire contracts.

Agreement was eventually reached

Above: 50050 returned to the main line in 1998, becoming the second Class 50 to operate on the national network in private ownership. Operated by DNLL, *Fearless* stands at Liverpool Street on 19 September 1999 having arrived with the 12.00 from Norwich, whilst working for Anglia Railways.   *Greg Edwards*

The life & times of 50050 *Fearless*

between Harry and DNLL to get 50050 re-registered for main line use, and it would then be used by the company on charters and for spot-hire use. However, after a very successful start to its operations, DNLL began to suffer from financial difficulties, following damage caused to one of the engines of newly-overhauled D9016, when oil in a collector drum caught fire on its first test run after overhaul.

Following its recertification for main line use, 50050 was used on a variety of workings during 1998 and 1999, before being taken out of use for a B-exam, which was never completed. Sadly for DNLL, after numerous problems, the company was forced to go into voluntary liquidation in 2004.

So does Harry regret the time that 50050 spent in the care of DNLL? "For the first three years it was in DNLL's care I was very happy with the arrangement. It was disappointing when the company started to get into difficulties, but I certainly can't say that I regret it. At the time it was the best situation for 50050 and without the work of DNLL, it would have remained at St Leonard's for a few more years. I liked the idea of joining forces with DNLL, as it was also a chance for me to get involved with 'Deltics', which were another favourite British locomotive type of mine."

One of the most prestigious workings for 50050 was hauling the luxurious Venice Simplon Orient Express trains, and Harry was fortunate enough to be able to sample this very special service, whilst being hauled by 50050, "It was great - one of the best moments of my life, being spoilt with fantastic food in a beautiful coach whilst being hauled by my own locomotive. The best moment for me on the VSOE was after arriving at London Victoria. Seeing the passengers walking past *Fearless* after an enjoyable journey filled me with immense pride."

Surprisingly though, prior to the VSOE train, he had only ever travelled on one train hauled by 50050, "I travelled behind *Fearless* from Exeter to Penzance, whilst it was in NSE livery. However, I did not manage to get on the service trains it worked in preservation, apart from the VSOE trip."

50050 has now not worked a train since 1999, but Harry explained this is mainly because components had been either stolen or swapped whilst it was in store. The theft of these parts left him wondering if it would ever haul a train again. So will 50050 be returned to the

First of the last

On 17 July 1999 50050 worked a railtour for NENTA railtours. Titled 'The Star Coast to Coast Explorer', the train worked from Felixstowe to Minehead, with a rake of Anglia Railways Mark 2 coaches. The train is pictured awaiting departure from Felixstowe. *Geoff Tibble*

main line in the future? Harry would like to see it back on the main line, but it is not a priority.

Following the DNLL collapse, Harry needed help getting 50050 back into to use and he made approaches to other Class 50 owning groups, to see if they would be interested in taking 50050 on, but no deal was forthcoming. Determined to get it back into traffic, Harry and some former DNLL volunteers founded the D400 Fund, to manage the restoration and look after the future of the locomotive.

Work by the D400 Fund began

Opposite: 50050 *Fearless* passes Hatton on 9 September 1998 working a Victoria to Stratford-upon-Avon Venice Simplon Orient Express British Pullman special and passing a pair of Centro Class 150/2 DMU's. For a short period at the end of the 1990s 50050 was used on a number of VSOE trains such as this. *Martin Loader*

whilst the locomotive was stored at Tyseley Locomotive Works, but in 2004 it was announced that 50050 would be moving to the Yeovil Railway Centre (YRC) - a small preservation centre, which seemed an unusual choice to many outsiders at the time it was moved there in 2004. However, Harry explains that the YRC had been keen for the locomotive to be based at Yeovil and also offered the possibility of covered accommodation in the future - something he believes is essential for the future wellbeing of the locomotive, especially as 50050's bodywork has suffered from years of outdoor storage.

The D400 Fund has been considerably assisted in recent years by volunteers connected with 50027 *Lion*, which is preserved on the North Yorkshire Moors Railway. Harry explained: "We got involved with the 50027 team by chance. But it is also a privately owned locomotive with its own dedicated group of people

around it. That's how I like it - a small dedicated group with a locomotive as its first priority, but keen to assist others where they can. That's the great thing about the preservation movement."

Despite being preserved for more than 15 years 50050 has never worked on a UK heritage railway. Harry says this isn't a deliberate plan and simply that 50050 was never invited to attend a heritage railway. Whilst it has been undergoing restoration at Yeovil, a number of enquiries have been received to run the locomotive at various heritage lines, but it will not be operated anywhere until its restoration has been fully completed.

It is clear that, despite some setbacks, Harry Schneider has no regrets about buying 50050 and with the work of the D400 Fund to revive it now well underway, the future for *Fearless* looks bright. Exciting times lie ahead for the pioneer Class 50.

Chapter 9
Back in action - the DNLL years

First of the last

Having been preserved in 1994 it would be four years before 50050 returned to main line service. The re-registered Class 50 was operated by Deltic 9000 Locomotive Limited for 18 months before being taken out of service. Former DNLL Chairman **MICHAEL TIMMS** tells how DNLL got involved in managing 50050's preserved main line career.

Saturday 3 May 1997 was the beginning of 50050's and Harry Schneider's association with Deltic 9000 Locomotives Limited (DNLL), and it all began with something of a chance meeting.

DNLL had taken our Class 55 'Deltic' D9016 *Gordon Highlander* to the open day at Crewe Electric Depot, as one of the many exhibits present. Our flagship locomotive - D9000 *Royal Scots Grey* - was regularly running on the mainline, and was unable to go to Crewe as it was due to haul the VSOE *The Railway Magazine* 'Centenary Pullman' from London Victoria to Bristol and back the following Bank Holiday Monday.

I remember walking into the open day site at Crewe and seeing 50050 *Fearless* as one of the main

exhibits in front of the shed. It was actually quite a surprise to see it on display, as until then it had spent almost all of its preserved life based out of the limelight at St Leonard's depot, and this was its first public appearance at any event away from its home base.

50050 had been purchased from BR at Plymouth Laira by Harry Schneider, and during the Crewe open day he got into conversation with DNLL engineer Chris Wayman about the requirements for mainline running. At the time D9000 was becoming very busy with railtour bookings and it was quickly becoming apparent that we could do with a second mainline registered locomotive as soon as possible, to cover for the possible non-availability of D9000, and also for what at that time was a

growing market for heritage traction on railtours.

After the open day had closed, Harry, Chris and the rest of the DNLL team who were present at the event met up for a meal and a review of the day's events. What transpired was a potential agreement to put 50050 back into mainline use alongside D9000. Following our initial conversations at Crewe, I travelled to Brussels with David Maxey, who was then our commercial director, to meet with Harry to discuss the way forward for the project.

Following tentative agreement to put 50050 under the DNLL umbrella, the locomotive was towed from St Leonard's to our operating base at Stewart's Lane on 9 July 1997 by 73129. The

Above: 50050 was reunited former railtour partner 50033 *Glorious* at the Crewe Electric Depot open day on 3 May 1997 - the first time the locomotives had been together since they had worked the 'Cornish Caper' railtour to York on 19 March 1994. This open day also marked the day that representatives of DNLL met with Harry Schneider and the scene was set for 50050 to return to main line use. *Geoff Tibble*
Left: On 17 July 1999 50050 hauls NENTA Traintours' 'The Star Coast to Coast Explorer' railtour away from Bristol Temple Meads station. *Martin Loader*

Back on the main line and in charge of a passenger train for the first time since hauling the '50 Terminator' railtour on 26 March 1994. For its preservation debut 50050 hauled a VSOE Pullman charter from Victoria to Southampton Docks on 5 August 1998. The inaugural train passes Eastleigh.   *Bob Foster*

internet went into overdrive, with some observers stating that 50050 was running under its own power, although it wasn't.

The formal agreement for the operation of 50050 under the auspices of DNLL was signed between ourselves and Harry Schneider over a fish and chip lunch at Penzance on 23 August 1997, following an astoundingly fast run trip down behind D9000 from Bristol with the Pathfinder Tours 'Duchy Deltic' railtour.

Once it had been safely delivered to Stewart's Lane, work began to bring 50050 up to the required standard for certification for mainline running by our Vehicle Acceptance Body, RESCO Railways. Unlike our own D9000, 50050 did not require a bogie overhaul before registration, but it did still require a host of other

jobs to be undertaken, including the replacement of its AWS equipment, air hoses, an oil change and thorough testing of all its safety related systems, before a test run could be arranged.

Finally, we were ready to take 50050 out for a test run to gain certification for mainline operation. DNLL's close relationship with VSOE at the time proved to be very useful for 50050, as the company kindly offered to assist us with the main line test run by loaning us the stock from their 'Ocean Liner Express' for the loaded test.

After much preparation, the test run operated by English Welsh & Scottish Railway (EWS) took place on the night of 1 April between Stewart's Lane depot and Swindon. To guard against the possible failure of 50050, back up

locomotive 47785 *Fiona Castle* was included in the train formation.

Unfortunately I wasn't able to go on this run, but I was kept fully informed of progress throughout. The journey to Swindon had been fairly slow due to pathing problems, but was without any serious defects with the '50'.

On arrival at Swindon it was found that the London end speedometer was not working. To avoid having to declare 50050 a failure, the defective speedometer was swapped over with that from the country end cab during the wait for the return path. The run home to Stewart's Lane proved to be much faster than the outward, which was just as well as we had to prove the locomotive was fit for 90mph running. All went well and once back at Stewart's Lane, RESCO pronounced that 50050

First of the last

was fit for the main line once again.

Having gained certification, we still had to gain confidence in the reliability of our newly registered locomotive. The chance of another non-passenger run to get some mileage under our belt with 50050 came during mid-May, when both D9000 and 50050 were invited to attend the South West Trains open days at Bournemouth TMD on 15 and 16 May.

It was arranged that 50050 would tow D9000 south on 14 May and back to London on 18 May. All went well with this run, and at Bournemouth 50050 was used as 'depot donkey' to shunt the exhibits in preparation for the event. The return run also went successfully, with D9000 in tow plus a support coach for the Merchant Navy Locomotive Preservation Society.

You would normally expect the first public run of a freshly certified locomotive to be an enthusiasts' special, but for 50050 it was to be a high profile trip, with a VSOE Pullman charter from Victoria to Southampton Docks on 5 August.

This trip was quite slackly timed, and possibly not suitable for a 'Deltic', so we decided to put 50050 on the run as a gentle start to its mainline career. Again, all went well to Southampton Docks, apart from a faulty headlight bulb which was replaced during the locomotive's visit to Eastleigh depot for fuel. 50050 then took the train back to Victoria in fine style, with a very happy and proud Harry Schneider on board.

It was not just Harry that was pleased with 50050, VSOE seemed impressed with it too. As a result the company booked the locomotive for three further days out starting with another run on the Pullmans - this time to Bristol on 2 September. One week later

there was trip to Stratford Upon Avon followed by a repeat of the Southampton Docks run on the 10th. It was on this latter working that celebrity chef Gary Rhodes was the guest chef on the train, leading to DNLL engineer Chris Wayman posing for photographs alongside Gary next to 50050's nameplate at Victoria station!

The first proper railtour that allowed enthusiasts the chance to ride behind the re-registered *Fearless* came on 26 September 1998, when railtour company Steamy Affairs hired the '50' to haul their 'Rose of the Shires' tour from Euston to Bescot and return. At Bescot, the steam part of the tour saw Stanier 5MT steam locomotive 45110 take over the train. On this tour 50050 actually passed D9000 on the mainline, which was on its way to Ramsgate with a Virgin Trains service - this being the first time that two preserved diesels from the same operator had met on the national network. After returning the train, its last in 1998 to Euston station, 50050 ran light diesel to Stewart's Lane having covered some 2,098 miles in its first year of main line running.

At the end of 1998, DNLL lost its

base at Stewart's Lane when EWS decided to lease the entire site to VSOE for its Pullman operations. This effectively made both D9000 and 50050 homeless. Luckily a home was offered to us by Anglia Railways at Norwich Crown Point Depot, which although not ideal for operating railtours, did at least give us a secure operating base. Following an initial movement to Stratford depot, 50050 was towed to Norwich by D9000.

Following the success of 50050 on the main line, DNLL looked for another Class 50 with which to pair it with. The final choice was 50002 *Superb*, based at the Paignton and Dartmouth Steam Railway and owned by the Devon Diesel Society. After reaching a loan agreement, DNLL despatched 50050 from Norwich to collect 50002 from its Devonshire home. On 14 December 1998, *Fearless* towed the NSE liveried *Superb* through familiar territory at Dawlish en-route to Norwich via an overnight stop at Willesden Depot.

The next day, the locomotives continued their journey to Crown Point in the company of two Anglia Railways Class 86s, which had been receiving attention

D9000 *Royal Scots Grey* was DNLL's flag carrier and became the first Class 55 Deltic to return to main line use in preservation. On 5 May 1997, D9000 heads the 'Centenary Pullman' for *The Railway Magazine* approaching Bapton Crossing.
Mark Few

at Willesden. The colourful entourage of 86215, 50050, 50002 and 86257 made its way along the Great Eastern main line on 15 December.

50050 didn't see any further activity until 25 March 1999, when it was booked to run light engine to Bounds Green in preparation for hauling a Pathfinder railtour the following day. The locomotive ran to Bounds Green for a planned move later that night to Bristol, where the tour was due to start at 04.30. The tour was a part-steam, part-diesel tour with 50050 booked to power the train to Crewe, where GWR 'King' 4-6-0 No. 6024 *King Edward I* would take the train forward to Carlisle and back.

Problems occurred however, and when the time came for 50050 to leave Bounds Green a battery fault had developed, leaving the locomotive unable to start. A series of hurried phone calls to EWS and Pathfinder resulted in a Class 47 taking the train to Crewe (although this locomotive - 47733 - also failed during the trip) whilst DNLL engineers worked to cure the battery fault on the '50'. As the return run from Crewe was not due to depart until 20.51 that evening, we had plenty of time to sort the problem. By late morning 50050 was up and running again, and after a few more phone calls to EWS it was arranged to move the locomotive light engine to Crewe to take up its booked return run later in the day. The run was successful, although the departure from Crewe was delayed after the tour had subsequently encountered problems with 6024 on Shap. After this run, 50050 was returned to Norwich.

Anglia Railways were now showing more interest in the possibility of using the Class 50 on some of its services. 50050's next run took place on 10 July, when it was used for a Norwich to Yarmouth shuttle service. Although only a light load of just three coaches, 50050 performed well, and we were hopeful of securing the rest of that summer's shuttle runs. Porterbrook Leasing subsequently offered 47825 for these duties free of charge, thus denying the '50' a useful revenue stream.

The following weekend, 17 July saw 50050 booked for another railtour, this time when NENTA Traintours ran from Felixstowe to Minehead and back, using a twelve coach Anglia Mk2 set of air-conditioned coaches including a Mk3 Buffet/restaurant. The train was top and tailed to Felixstowe with 47825 taking the train in as empty coaching stock, with 50050 on the rear so that it would be at the correct end for a departure to the West.

This was to be 50050's biggest adventure so far, with Chris Wayman giving up his usual position on D9000 - which was running to Ramsgate the same day - so he could look after 50050.

The train ran from Felixstowe, via Ipswich, to the Great Western mainline, then via Slough, Wootton Bassett, Weston-super-Mare and on to the West Somerset Railway for the last section of the journey to Minehead. Again, all seemed to be going well with 50050 arriving on time at the end of the outward journey.

The return to Felixstowe was also without problems, until the very last leg at Hatfield Peverel when 50050 suddenly split an oil hose, and managed to lose most of its oil on the engine room bedplate, resulting in an instant shut down. Luckily, 47825 was not too far away and was sent to tow the errant Class 50 and its train to Felixstowe. 50050 was soon towed back to Norwich, where it was quickly repaired and given new oil.

Anglia Railways decided to use *Fearless* on a scheduled service train in the same way that it had previously used D9000. The train chosen was a Norwich to London Liverpool Street service, but it was marketed as having 'special' motive power. And so 19 September 1999 turned out to be 50050's one and only long distance trip for Anglia Railways, and is currently its last passenger run on the main line.

Thankfully 50050 behaved impeccably on this run and Anglia Railways was very pleased with the event. There was to be no repeat however, as changes to the operating rules being made by the Rolling Stock Acceptance Board would make it much more difficult for any Train Operating Company (TOC) to use Class 50s or 'Deltics' on service trains unless the locomotives were formally included that TOC's Safety Case.

Virgin Trains did not have such a problem however, and was still able to use D9000 as the 'Deltic' had been included in its Safety Case. The introduction of the new 'Voyager' units in place of locomotive-hauled trains meant that DNLL's spot hire work with Virgin Trains was coming to an end anyway.

At the end of 1999, the DNLL locomotives again required a new home after being given notice to quit Norwich Crown Point depot. West Coast Traincare kindly offered 50002 and 50050 accommodation at Wembley depot ahead of being included in a plan to use Class 50s on WCML 'Thunderbird' duties - their idea, not ours. So on 20 December, 50050 towed 50002 from Norwich to Stratford, for onward

Opposite: 50050 *Fearless* snakes through the Wylye Valley at Great Wishford with the 09.45 Victoria - Bristol VSOE special train on 2 September 1998.

Martin Loader

transfer to Wembley the following day.

The two locomotives were parked next to the WCML for the next seven months. At this time DNLL was entering into a partnership with Fragonset Railways, who had promised to maintain DNLL's fleet on its own Maintenance and Overhaul Policy. The downside of this arrangement was that Fragonset prevented DNLL engineers gaining access to the locomotives. Although D9000 was operated for a while by Fragonset, the Class 50s were stored without covers on their exhausts, resulting in water contamination to the engines. 50050 was however, successfully accessed by DNLL staff who managed to bar the engine over.

Both 50050 and 50002 were moved from Wembley to Old Oak Common depot for display at the Open Day on 5 August 2000. Fragonset then announced that both the locomotives would be moved to its base at Barrow Hill after the event. This was not our first choice of a home for them in view of the location and further outside storage. The move to Barrow Hill took place and both '50s' remained in the open, without covers on the exhausts.

During summer 2001, Fragonset announced that they intended to use 50050 on one of their own railtours from Derby to Paignton and back in August 2001. Both DNLL and Harry Schneider were unhappy about the level of preparation of the Class 50. Although 50050 was given a partial exam and run up and down at Barrow Hill, with the date of the railtour moving closer, an urgent meeting was arranged with Fragonset to discuss our concerns. At this meeting, DNLL decided to withdraw all of its locomotives from Fragonset's care and the agreement between the two organisations came to an end. This resulted in D9000 running to Barrow Hill on 23 November 2001 to collect 50050 and move it to Tyseley, where restoration to working order could begin again.

D9000 continued to operate with DNLL until it was withdrawn due to a generator fault in 2002. D9016 was then available to take its place on the mainline, but work on 50050 was placed in the hands of a group of DNLL engineers at Tyseley, who after the demise of DNLL in 2004, went on to form the D400 Fund, which still looks after the locomotive today.

Chapter 10
Enter the D400 Fund

Richard Thompson

50050's restoration at Yeovil Railway Centre is being managed by the D400 Fund. **RICHARD THOMPSON** tells the story about how the Fund was founded, and some of the challenges faced with the ongoing restoration of the locomotive.

The D400 Fund was formed in 2003, as a result of a chance encounter with the owner of 50050 at Cambridge in December 2002. I was on-board 'Deltic' D9016, on the first train to be operated by Merlin Rail and during the journey DNLL chairman Michael Timms received a phone call from Harry Schneider. After arrival in London Liverpool Street, we went light engine to Cambridge to stable D9016 after its trip.

By chance, Harry was about to drive through Cambridge on his way to catch the ferry at Harwich back to The Netherlands, where he lives. We arranged to meet up in the town centre to discuss the future welfare of 50050. Harry said that he was concerned about the condition of 50050, which had

stood out of use for more than three years and stated he wanted to see his '50' run again if at all possible. Michael and Harry asked if I would be willing to go and take a look at the condition of the locomotive. Despite having initially not being too keen on DNLL having any involvement in the operation of Class 50s, I agreed to go an inspect 50050, as I really wanted to help out the friendly Dutchman with the English Electric locomotive.

And so, on a freezing cold day at the end of January 2003, I made my way to Tyseley Locomotive Works to survey 50050 - well, as much as was possible without starting it. It had been withdrawn by DNLL at the end of 1999, as it needed its annual Resco Railways safety examination and was also

due to undergo a B-exam. 50050 had received some attention from Fragonset Railways whilst stabled at Barrow Hill, but the exact nature of work done to it had not been recorded.

Surprisingly, 50050 was in relatively good condition and the engine barred over freely. The downsides from the inspection were a set of flat batteries, the fire bottles had been discharged and all of its AWS equipment had been swapped with equipment that appeared to be so old it would have been out of date during the BR railtour program in the early 1990s. Perhaps the most worrying discovery was that the spare electronic components Harry had purchased for the locomotive, and which had been stored on board, were missing.

First of the last

Following the initial inspection, the decision was made to carry out sufficient work towards being able to start the locomotive, as this would reveal much more information on the overall condition of it than any static inspection ever could. After some remedial work 50050 was started on 12 March 2003.

Throughout 2003, DNLL had regular contract work hauling empty coaching stock from the Mid Hants Railway to London and back again in the evening. This working was restricted to 45mph, due to a steam locomotive being in the consist and would have been a much more suitable working for a Class 50 than a 'Deltic'. The initial plan was to try and get 50050 ready to haul these trains as soon as possible and we would worry about sprucing up the rather faded and worn paintwork on the locomotive at a later date.

The first jobs tackled saw efforts made to try and sort out a low power fault and to resolve problems that appeared to have surfaced with 50050's KV10 electronic control board. A number of time-expired items were replaced and new AWS equipment, fire bottles and buffer beam air hoses were also fitted, as we worked to revive *Fearless*.

While work continued on the restoration, it was decided 50050 needed its own bank account to manage the finances. This would speed up getting funds from Harry Schneider directly to 50050, without having to go via the main DNLL account. This is how the D400 Fund was born and at this stage there was no intention, or even desire, for the D400 Fund to become the custodians of 50050. It was simply set up to manage the restoration money.

In the Summer of 2004 and after a problematical few months DNLL ceased trading. Harry and I

discussed the situation and all possible options were considered to ensure the wellbeing of 50050. Other '50' owning groups were contacted to see if they wanted to take it on alongside their own locomotives - most either never replied, or said they weren't really interested. There was also not much of a market for second-hand Class 50s, so selling the locomotive was not a viable option - certainly not a sale that would have recouped the expenditure that Harry had spent on it.

Even though it might seem a slightly unrealistic proposal, scrapping the locomotive was also considered. With so many other '50s' preserved, the component parts would have attracted a premium price and there is no doubt that scrapping 50050 would have been the best financial option for all concerned. However, it was readily accepted that 50050 is no ordinary Class 50. As the first member of English Electric's final design of mixed traffic locomotive, the eventual decision was that it was far too important to face a cutters torch ten years after it ended its career with British Rail.

With all other options now discounted we were left with one remaining option - to go it alone and get 50050 back into a serviceable condition, although it would be unlikely that it would be returned to main line service. It was explained to Harry that because of the stolen or swapped parts, it would be a rather long and complicated restoration project, unless we could source the missing components. This task was made that much more difficult as some of the replacement parts were very difficult to find.

The first job for a newly independent D400 Fund was to explain the situation to our hosts at Tyseley Locomotive Works. Thankfully they were sympathetic and helpful when we explained our plight, and if the locomotive had not already been promised a home at the Yeovil Railway Centre (YRC), we probably would have asked to stay in Birmingham.

Many people have asked why such a large locomotive like a Class 50 is based at a railway centre with only a short running line. The simple answer is that they asked if they could have it. YRC, adjacent to Yeovil Junction Station, had for

12 March 2003 and 50050 comes back to life, after more than three years in storage out of use. It would be a further six years before repairs allowed it to move under its own power. *Richard Thompson*

a long time sought a Class 50 as an exhibit. '50s' had passed through Yeovil many times during their working lives and 50050 would have passed through Yeovil Junction on a regular basis - even whilst working the farewell tour back in March 1994. YRC had previously offered a home to both 50027 and 50033. I got to know the people from YRC when Merlin Railways deposited D9016 at the centre following the movement of 50002 from Barrow Hill to the South Devon Railway on 24 September 2003.

The YRC provided an excellent home to D9016, in its undercover shed. A month later, on 30 October 2003, I was back at YRC, but this time it was to take D9016 on what would be DNLL's final outing on the mainline - a light engine trip to Southall. Discussing the situation with 50050 on the platform while awaiting departure, YRC offered it a permanent home. Fragonset Railways kindly

sponsored the move of the locomotive and, on 15 October 2004, 31601 took 50050 on the first leg of a two day journey from Tyseley to Westbury. Just after departing Tyseley 50050 made what was likely to have been its last ever visit to Birmingham New Street station. The journey was completed the following day with a short trip from Westbury to Yeovil Junction.

After 50050 arrived at Yeovil, we were contacted by a man I had got to know at Clapham Junction station, when I had been on D9016. He had been filming and I was waiting for a green signal. Keith Robertson was a friend of 50027's owner, Mike Fuller. Keith said that 50027 had developed a speedometer fault and parts were needed quickly, or it would not be able to take part in that year's diesel gala. We were pleased to be able to help by offering to loan the required parts from 50050. This was the start of a partnership that

has seen both groups work together for the benefit of both Class 50s.

We were delighted when 50050 took power and moved for the first time in nine years on 24 June 2009. Restoration work continues to return 50050 to the best possible condition and we hope eventually that it will occasionally venture away from Yeovil once restoration has been completed.

One aspect of the restoration that has proved to be especially challenging is in repairing damage to the KV10 control unit inside 50050, which almost deserves a chapter on its own. Here is the story of our problematical KV10.

Shortly after we had started work on the locomotive in 2003, a friend telephoned me and said "*You are wasting your time with that '50'. It will always have low power, as it's been put beyond restoration*", suggesting that the '50' had been

Although the locomotive has spent the last couple of years looking rather unkempt, work has been concentrated on internal restoration work, with bodywork repairs being done in 2010, prior to the locomotive being repainted. *Andrew Fuller*

deliberately sabotaged. I knew that DNLL had been rather unpopular with some people in the railway world and many had thought the 'Deltics' should be sold. However, 50050 was privately owned and this sort of activity was beyond the pale.

Once we had started 50050 in March 2003, the problems started to come to light. After warming up and showing good oil pressure, everything seemed to work well and the decision was taken to see if it would move under its own power. The reversers and contactors worked, and the amp meter rose - but only just. About 300 amps was all it would produce. After months of testing and having taken advice from various people about the cause of the problem, the fault was traced to the KV10, also known as the CU3 field supply unit.

There had always seemed something rather odd about 50050's KV10. As one of Laira's railtour '50s', it was lavishly treated by depot staff. The electrical cubicle looked like new and it was in excellent condition. The exception was the traction KV10. It was rather scruffy in its appearance. There were also labels on all the wires attaching it to the locomotive. This suggested it had been removed and refitted at some stage and it didn't look like it belonged with all the other more-immaculate components in the cubicle.

Enquiries revealed that nobody at DNLL, or Fragonset Railways, had removed or touched the KV10 during the time they operated it. Why would they? 50050 was in full working order while in the care of both companies. Nobody involved with it remembered the labels on the KV10 wiring. Harry Schneider stated that he was sure they weren't there when he bought the locomotive. The suspect KV10 was removed and sent to St Leonards for inspection.

The answer came back that this was not the KV10 fitted to 50050 during its time at St Leonards in the mid-1990s and prior to its main line re-certification in 1998.

We knew 50050 had been broken into and the spares stolen. The AWS equipment had been swapped too. 50050's KV10 had been stolen and a defective one had been fitted in its place. With no spare available and having discovered the last place in the country that overhauled them had closed, 50050 was facing a bleak future. We would need to repair or replace the defective KV10 to stand any chance of letting it run under its own power again.

Eventually we were fortunate enough to be able to buy a spare KV10. When we fitted it to 50050 however, it actually proved to be in worse condition than the one we already had. As the years went on, we investigated several options. Initially we looked into the possibility of sharing a KV10 with 50027, then considered persuading a gentleman who used to overhaul KV10s to come out of retirement, or even buying another Class 50 - just for its KV10!

We knew it wasn't possible to test a KV10 away from the locomotive, as the Swindon test rig had long since been dismantled. Various companies offered to overhaul the KV10 for us, but they all admitted they had not done one before. Not keen to be the guinea pig, we were left with one option - dismantle it ourselves to see if any damage was evident.

In the summer of 2008, former Laira depot electrician Dickie Daw dismantled the KV10 unit. Testing with a multi-meter and a home made test rig, everything checked out and the thyristors were fired successfully. Then we came across two zena diodes, which were burnt out and one was detached

from its mounting base. At long last it appeared we had found the problem. This confirmed our view that key parts had been switched over, leaving 50050 with inferior equipment.

Tracing the faulty zenas proved difficult and we needed help from an electronics expert. This led to our KV10 being sent to a workshop near York, but the prognosis was not good. We were advised that the replacement parts needed were no longer commercially available, and 50050's future as a working locomotive was again looking bleak. The only option was to despatch our spare KV10 and hope its diodes were still in a serviceable condition. A short time later our two KV10s returned - one had been repaired and was now hopefully serviceable, but the other was still in a sorry state.

At Yeovil, the unit was refitted and the wires checked to see if they were in the correct place. It was a tense, nervous moment when on 24 July 2009, Andy Fuller put the controller into forward and selected notch one on the power handle. After a few seconds the amp meter jumped up and stayed there. Subject to lots of testing, our KV10 nightmare was over. Thankfully other tasks required in the restoration of 50050 shouldn't prove to be quite so challenging.

One of the cabs of 50050 awaiting restoration a the Yeovil Railway Centre. *Richard Thompson*

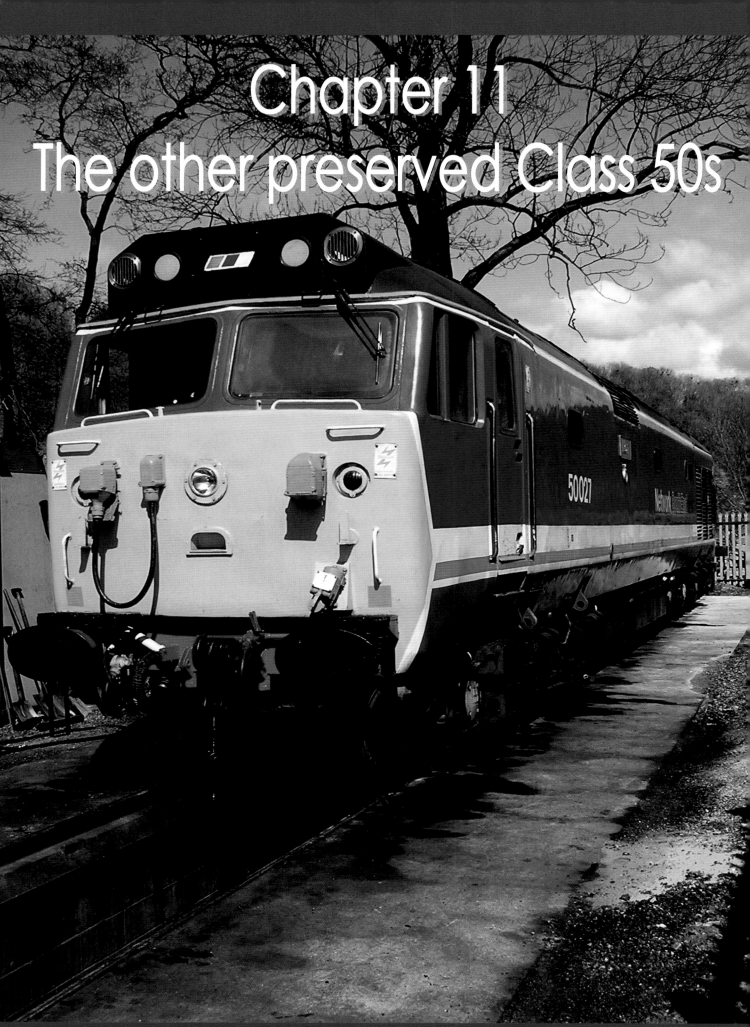

Chapter 11
The other preserved Class 50s

First of the last

The withdrawal from service of 50011 *Centurion* in February 1987 marked the beginning of the end for the Class 50, with a steady trickle of withdrawals over the next three years. By 1990, the writing was well and truly on the wall for the '50s', with BR seemingly keen to rundown the class at an increasingly rapid rate.

The Class 50s had long been popular with railway enthusiasts and it was inevitable that some would survive by being purchased for restoration. Modern traction preservation was growing in popularity in the early 1990s, with many heritage railways understanding the benefit of diesel traction as an alternative for steam.

In spring 1991 BR announced that three Class 50s were to be offered for sale to preservationists by tender, with 50008 *Thunderer*, 50019 *Ramillies* and 50035 *Ark Royal* being the locomotives selected for disposal. At the time 50008 was still in service on a restricted basis as one of Laira's dedicated railtour locomotives along with 50015 *Valiant*, but both 50019 and 50035 had already been withdrawn.

Shortly afterwards, BR decided to remove 50008 from the tender, leaving the other two locomotives to be sold. After the tender list had closed, BR announced that 50035 had been secured for preservation by the Fifty Fund. The locomotive was handed over to its new owners by the then Network SouthEast Managing Director Chris Green at the Old Oak Common Open Day on Saturday 16 August 1991. The first Class 50 had been secured for preservation at a cost of £16,500. After the event, 50035 was moved to St Leonard's depot.

The second '50' up for disposal, 50019, also found salvation, being purchased by the Class 50 Locomotive Association and it subsequently moved to the Tunbridge Wells and Eridge Railway for restoration to working order.

At the time, what couldn't be envisaged is just how popular the locomotives would be with diesel preservationists. Although three Class 50s - 50023 *Howe*, 50040 *Leviathan* and 50043 *Eagle* - subsequently ended up being scrapped, there are still a healthy 18 examples surviving in 2010 and at the time of writing 12 preserved '50s' are either serviceable or very close to returning to use.

50002 *Superb*
Owner: Devon Diesel Society

50002 holds a place in railway preservation history for being the first privately owned Class 50 to be started up by its new post-BR owners. This took place at the locomotive's new home on the Paignton & Dartmouth Steam Railway (P&DSR), shortly after it arrived there in February 1992.

Now owned by the Devon Diesel

Above: In 2006 50031 & 50049 worked service trains for Arriva Trains Wales. 50049 is seen at Fishguard Harbour on 28 August 2006. **Andy Coward**

Society, 50002 was quickly restored to BR blue livery and given back its former identity of 402. The locomotive was a regular performer on the P&DSR until it was moved away to Norwich Crown Point depot by DNLL in 2000, with the intention that it would be re-registered for main line running.

As detailed in Chapter 9 however, this never happened and 50002 was eventually returned to the DDS. Unfortunately, during the four years it was out of service, its

Opposite: 50027 *Lion* is now based on the North Yorkshire Moors Railway and is the only preserved Class 50 to retain revised Network SouthEast livery.
Andy Fuller
Above: One of the first Class 50s to be secured for preservation was 50019 *Ramillies*, which is now based on the Mid Norfolk Railway.
Andy Coward

Work is now well underway on the mechanical and bodywork overhaul of 50002 *Superb* on the South Devon Railway. The locomotive, which is being cosmetically returned to as-built condition as D402 is pictured on display at Buckfastleigh in October 2009. ***Martin Hart***

condition had deteriorated and 50002 now required extensive mechanical and bodywork attention before it could be returned to operational condition.

The DDS relocated 50002 to a new home on the South Devon Railway at Buckfastleigh, where it was delivered by D9016 *Gordon Highlander* in September 2003.

Whilst it is still to be returned to service, 50002 has undergone a high quality bodywork overhaul during which it was restored externally to 'as-built' condition and renumbered as D402. A similar makeover had previously been carried out on D444 *Exeter* by the Fifty Fund. At this time it is not known when D402 will return to service.

50007 *Sir Edward Elgar*
Owner: Privately owned by members of Class 40 Appeal

Withdrawn at the end of March 1994 along with 50050 following the '50 Terminator' railtour, 50007 was kept in secure storage at Laira depot before being offered for sale that same summer.

The locomotive was purchased by three members of the Class 40 Appeal - owners of 40012 *Aureol* at the Midland Railway Centre (MRC). 50007 was also to be based at the MRC, where it went into service shortly after arriving.

In preservation, 50007 has retained its unique Great Western Railway style green livery, in spite of repeated calls for the locomotive to be restored to blue livery with *Hercules* nameplates. The '50' has been fitted with a set of snowploughs, which it never carried in its BR days, and the name and number plates have been painted with a red

background on occasions.

50007 has visited a number of heritage railways since entering preservation, including the Great Central Railway, where it remains at the time of writing having arrived there in October 2009.

50008 *Thunderer*
Owner: Privately owned
Purchased in the autumn of 1992 by rail enthusiast and record producer Pete Waterman, 50008 was moved to the East Lancashire Railway (ELR) at Bury, where it was delivered that October. The locomotive hauled its first train in preservation on the same day it arrived, following an examination and testing.

50008 remained on the ELR for one year and it was repainted in large logo livery on one side only for a filming contract.

First of the last

Mr Waterman aimed to return his locomotive to mainline service and it was subsequently moved to the London and North Western Railway (LNWR) workshops at Crewe for an overhaul. Little work was actually carried out however, and 50008 was later offered for sale along with a number of other locomotives from the Waterman collection, which were disposed of in 1996.

The future for 50008 brightened when it was purchased by luxury train operator Venice Simplon Orient Express (VSOE) with a view to hauling its Pullman services across the country. Still located at Crewe, the work on its overhaul was restarted.

With the overhaul progressing well, VSOE's parent company Sea Containers, then decided that 50008 was not required for VSOE services and that it would be prepared for use in Peru instead. During its overhaul, 50008 received an overhauled pair of bogies and a zero-hours power unit. Not required for use in Peru, the locomotive's vacuum brakes and AWS equipment were removed.

Sea Containers later abandoned its plans to send to 50008 to Peru and the overhaul was stopped. It remained in store at Crewe until it was sold again, this time to Hanson Traction (HT) in 2007.

The locomotive's long running overhaul was finally completed in 2009 and it was moved to HT's base at Wansford on the Nene Valley Railway (NVR). The owner intends to return 50008 to the mainline in the future but this will require the fitting of Train Protection & Warning System (TPWS) and On Train Monitoring & Recording (OTMR) equipment.

Now back in working order, 50008 worked its first trains in more than 16 years at the NVR in October 2009. The locomotive

Former Laira celebrity 50007 *Sir Edward Elgar* is now owned by the Class 40 Appeal. The GWR green '50' has recently visited the Great Central Railway and is seen running round its train at Leicester North on 11 September 2009. *Martin Hart*

then returned to the ELR for its diesel event before undergoing a repaint into the Laira style blue livery it carried prior to withdrawal in 1992.

50015 *Valiant*
Owner: Bury Valiant Group
For its final year in BR service, 50015 often worked in multiple with 50008 as Laira's two dedicated railtour locomotives - prior to their withdrawal from service in 1992. It was fitting then that 50015 should also be purchased for preservation by Pete Waterman, and it was delivered to the ELR with 50008 in October 1992, before entering service the same day.

Mr Waterman also sold 50015 in 1996 and it was bought by the Manchester Class Fifty Group, which had looked after it since it had arrived at the ELR. Following a number of years in service, the locomotive underwent an extensive bodywork overhaul and was repainted in large logo blue livery.

By 2003 however, 50015 required attention to a defective traction motor and various other smaller repairs, and it was taken out of

traffic. Years later and with interest in it seemingly waning, 50015 was still out of service at Bury, with many observers doubting whether it would survive.

Behind the scenes, several active members of the ELR were making plans to buy the locomotive. In the autumn of 2007, it was confirmed that 50015 had been sold to a consortium of ELR members - now known as the Bury Valiant Group.

In spite of having been out of service for more than four years, 50015 was quickly returned to service and hauled trains on the ELR in December 2007. The locomotive still requires a body lift however, to address the defective traction motor which is currently isolated.

In late 2009, 50015 was taken out of service to allow further bodywork repairs to be carried out. Some mechanical repairs were made at the same time and the locomotive was repainted in large logo livery. While many enthusiasts are keen to see 50015 back in its grey and yellow 'Dutch' livery - as carried in its final year of BR service, its owners have so far resisted. They have stated however, that *Valiant* will once again be painted in the celebrated livery in the future.

50017 *Royal Oak*
Owner: Privately owned

Having been purchased by enthusiast Dr John Kennedy following its withdrawal in 1991, 50017 was initially taken to Crewe Heritage Centre for restoration work to begin.

After several years at Crewe, the locomotive was moved to the West Somerset Railway (WSR), where it joined 50149 *Defiance*, which was based on the WSR at the time. Work to restore 50017 was completed in 1998 and it was painted in Railfreight triple grey colours to match 50149, with the newly restored '50' being renumbered 50117.

50017's time as a working locomotive on the WSR was short-lived and agreement was reached for it to return to mainline service, hauling luxury dining trains for VSOE. Following mainline certification, the locomotive returned to service in 2000 and was painted into London, Midland & Scottish Railway maroon livery with gold stripes - the repaint being carried out by Riley & Son (E) Ltd at Bury on the ELR. After hauling many trains for VSOE, the agreement to use 50017 was cancelled and the locomotive was sidelined at Tyseley Locomotive Works.

Following several years out of service at Tyseley, 50017 was put up for sale by its owner who wanted to concentrate on the other locomotives in his collection.

In summer 2009, 50017 was sold to Dave Cunningham who moved it to the Plym Valley Railway in Plymouth - close to its former home of Laira depot. The new owner quickly returned 50017 to operational condition, and it moved under its own power for the first time in nearly a decade in November 2009. At the time of writing, a repaint into early NSE style livery is planned.

50019 *Ramillies*
Owner: Class 50 Locomotive Association

The second Class 50 to be taken into private ownership was 50019, which was bought in September 1991 by the Class 50 Locomotive Association, having been one of the first three Class 50s listed on a BR tender list.

50019 had been withdrawn by BR In September 1990 following a main generator flashover. The new home for 50019 was chosen as the embryonic Tunbridge Wells and Eridge Railway - the newly preserved locomotive arriving

Two preserved Class 50s that have been out of the limelight for some time are 50017 *Royal Oak* and 50021 *Rodney*, which were both stored at Tyseley Locomotive Works when pictured in February 2005. 50017 has since been sold and moved to the Plym Valley Railway.
Martin Hart

there on 7 January 1992 for restoration work to begin.

Restoration work continued at Eridge to bring 50019 back into working order, but in May 1999 it was moved to a new home on the pro-diesel Mid Norfolk Railway (MNR), where it has remained ever since. 50019 was employed on shunting duties at its new home within hours of being delivered to the railway and entered passenger service shortly afterwards.

After initially running in BR blue colours, 50019 was repainted into large logo blue in 2004. Although it has had spells out of use for maintenance and repairs, 50019 has remained a regular and consistent performer on the MNR.

50021 *Rodney*
Owner: 50021 Association
50021 was one of the Class 50s stored at Stratford depot following withdrawal. Although it had been subjected to some component recovery, when it was placed on the tender list the locomotive was found to be in much better condition than had been previously thought.

After being purchased by the 50021 Association, *Rodney* was moved to the Gloucestershire & Warwickshire Railway (GWR) at Toddington, where restoration work was carried out. After spending several years on the GWR, the locomotive was moved to the Bo'ness and Kinneil Railway in Scotland - the most northerly base for any of the preserved Class 50s.

50027 *Lion* has been based at the North Yorkshire Moors Railway since 1994 and has retained revised NSE colours throughout its preservation career. 50027 stands at Goathland in fading evening light with an evening dining train on 20 September 2008. *Ian Horner*

In 2000 however, while being used as a carriage heater 50021 suffered a serious ETH generator failure - leading to more than two years in store at Bo'ness. In 2002 the locomotive was moved to Tyseley Locomotive Works, where it has remained since.

An extensive bodywork and mechanical overhaul has been started, but a return to service is still a long way off at the time of writing. A recent development has seen the Association take over the responsibility for looking after 50033 *Glorious* and at the present time, this locomotive is taking priority.

50023 *Howe* (scrapped)
Owner: Privately owned
50023 was one of nine heavily stripped Class 50s bought for scrap by CF Booth in 1991. Shortly after being delivered by rail to Rotherham, it was sold - along with 50001/040/045 to the engineering charity Operation Collingwood, which aimed to re-engineer the locomotives using modern components with the work being carried out by apprentices.

In spite of some initial success, Operation Collingwood failed to move any of its '50s' from Booth's and they were re-sold to the scrap merchant, who then offered them for sale to preservationists. The derelict 50023 was purchased by a private individual, who aimed to restore it to working order.

The locomotive was moved the short distance to the Barrow Hill Roundhouse, near Chesterfield, arriving in June 2000. The owner quickly stripped 50023 of its major components, including the damaged power unit - originally used inside DP2.

A start was made on bodywork repairs with a view to returning the locomotive to original condition as D423. Progress was made with No.2 end cab but restoration of such a derelict locomotive was never going to be easy and the work slowed considerably.

The end for 50023 came in 2004 when the owner decided he would be unable to complete the project. The locomotive was sold to the Harry Needle Railroad Company (also based at Barrow Hill). After the recovery of spare parts by other Class 50 owners, the remains of 50023 were scrapped on site at Barrow Hill in March 2004.

The story of 50026 *Indomitable* is one of the most remarkable of the preserved Class 50s. Bought for scrap by CF Booth it was subsequently purchased as a source of spares for 50027 *Lion* before being sold to Paul Spracklen who has rebuilt the locomotive over a period of 17 years.

Both: Martin Hart

50026 *Indomitable*
Owner: Privately owned

The story of 50026 is nothing short of remarkable. As with 50023, it was bought in a heavily stripped condition for scrap by CF Booth, and delivered to its Rotherham scrap yard in 1992.

Booth's had long supported the efforts of preservationists and the owners of 50027 had looked at all the '50s' at Rotherham with a view to buying one as a source of spares for their locomotive. The decision was taken to buy 50026 along with some components from the other '50s', and in April 1993 the locomotive left Rotherham for its new home at Ropley on the Mid Hants Railway (MHR).

50026 had not been on the MHR for very long when 50027 left the railway for an eventual new home in North Yorkshire. 50026 was then sold to Paul Spracklen, who had a long term aim to restore it to operational status.

Mr Spracklen arranged for his new acquisition to be housed on the Ministry of Defence rail network at Bicester. Here he steadily began the task of stripping 50026 down, before overhauling the components and rebuilding the locomotive over the next 15 years.

Fate was to deal 50026 a cruel

blow in October 2004 however, when the locomotive's bodyshell was dropped during a lifting exercise by a Territorial Army squadron at Bicester. Thankfully, as the power unit and other internal components were not fitted at the time - damage sustained was not as severe as it could have been, but the ensuing claim against the MoD held-up the restoration for around three years.

In 2007, 50026 was moved to Rail Vehicle Engineering Ltd's workshops in Derby where bodywork repairs were carried out. With restoration work restarted, the power unit was lowered into place and the locomotive was repainted in large logo livery, before being moved to Old Oak Common depot where work continued.

In April 2009, 50026 was started for the first time in nearly 19 years

- at its former home depot. Soon afterwards, the locomotive was moved with 50035 to Eastleigh Works. Due to the Crossrail project, Old Oak Common had to be vacated and the site was being cleared of all locomotives and rolling stock.

50026 made its first public appearance in preservation at the Eastleigh Works 100 years event, held over the weekend of 22-24 May 2009. After the event, it was moved via another open day at Long Marston to the Severn Valley Railway (SVR) - where it is to be based when not working on the mainline. A number of problems with the locomotive however, prevented it from taking part in the SVR diesel gala in October 2009 - at which it was to have been one of the star attractions.

Further problems in 2010 led to a planned appearance at the

Swanage Railway in May being postponed, and Mr Spracklen announcing that 50026 would be unlikely to return to service until 2011. The locomotive has since returned to Eastleigh Works for fitting of TPWS and OTMR equipment ahead of being registered for use on the mainline. The owner still hopes to return 50026 to mainline use towards the end of 2011.

50027 *Lion*
Owner: Privately owned

50027 was bought privately by Mike Fuller in 1992, who moved the locomotive to the MHR, where it arrived on 10 March the same year. Following a battery overhaul, the locomotive was started for the first time in preservation on 12 April. Further attention was required to the cylinder liners and pistons - some of which required replacement, before 50027 could re-enter service.

50008 *Thunderer* has had an interesting time since it was preserved in 1992 by Pete Waterman. Originally a mainline overhaul was planned before it was sold to VSOE for use on the 'Northern Belle' and at one stage VSOE wanted to export it to Peru. Now owned by Hanson Traction, it was repainted into Laira Blue whilst visiting the East Lancashire Railway in 2010. 50008 stands at Ramsbottom on 13 March 2010.   *Ian Horner*

On 17 May 1992, the immaculate 50027 entered service on the MHR, becoming the third '50' to work in preservation. At the end of the year, Mr Fuller bought 50026 as a source of spares for 50027 and moved it down to the MHR in April 1993.

A dispute between the MHR and the locomotives' owning group however, led to both 50026 and 50027 being asked to leave the railway. As described above, 50026 was sold to Paul Spracklen, while 50027 initially departed to attend an open day at Exeter in May 1994. By the end of 1994 it had taken up an invitation to visit the North Yorkshire Moors Railway (NYMR), but its arrival at Grosmont was too late to work any trains that year.

50027 entered service on the NYMR on 6 May 1995 and immediately proved to be a popular attraction - although its NSE livery contrasted sharply with the other locomotives based on the line. Such was the success of its visit, 50027 has remained on the railway based at Grosmont, for nearly 16 years and has proved to be a reliable performer.

50029 *Renown*
Owner: Renown Repulse Restoration Group
As one of the final Class 50s left in normal service, the end for 50029 came in March 1992 after a severe engine failure two months earlier. It would be another ten years however, before 50029 could be regarded as preserved.

Following purchase by Operation Collingwood, 50029 and 50030 became the final Class 50s to leave Laira depot when they were moved to Allied Steel and Wire at Cardiff in 1994. The locomotives were later moved to the Pontypool and Blaenavon Railway for further storage.

With no work taking place on either locomotive over the next few years, the P&BR wanted them moved away. In the summer of 2002, the trustees of Operation Collingwood abandoned plans to rebuild 50029 and 50030 and offered the pair for sale.

Although subject to component recovery by BR and unofficial parts removal while in store, both locomotives were in much better condition than the other Operation Collingwood '50s' based at Rotherham.

The pair was being eyed by existing Class 50 owners for spares supply but a new group - the Renown Repulse Restoration Group (RRRG) - was hastily set up and submitted a bid for both locomotives. The RRRG bid was successful and included a recovered cab from 50037 *Illustrious*. The group stated that its intention was to restore both '50s' to working condition.

First of the last

Opposite Page: After its final workings at the North Yorkshire Moors Railway in August 2004, 50033 was transferred to STEAM, where it was displayed undercover at the museum. However, three years later it moved to Tyseley Locomotive Works and at the time of writing is being returned to working order by the 50021 Association. *Martin Hart*

Right: 50033 worked its final trains on the NYMR at a special farewell running day on 14 August 2004 and departs from New Bridge with a suitable headboard for the occasion. *Ian Horner*

Both locomotives were moved to Peak Rail at Rowsley in 2002, but 50029 was deemed to be in poorer condition and it was stored, while attention was focussed on 50030. The RRRG did carry out a bodywork overhaul on 50029 however, before painting it in large logo livery, with a black roof.

Restoration to full working order is still an aspiration of the RRRG, but at the time of writing 50029 remains stored at Rowsley South and it is viewed as a long-term project.

50030 *Repulse*
Owner: Renown Repulse Restoration Group
Aside from the dedicated railtour locomotives, 50030 was the final Class 50 to be taken out of service - following a main generator failure in February 1992. It was officially withdrawn in April.

50030's post-withdrawal story matches that of 50029 and after purchase by the RRRG, the locomotive was moved to its new home at Peak Rail, Rowsley.

The RRRG carried out a bodywork overhaul on 50030 before painting it in large logo livery, ahead of switching attention to the mechanical and electrical restoration of the locomotive.

Work is now reaching an advanced stage, and the RRRG hopes to have 50030 operational again within the next two years.

50031 *Hood*
Owner: Privately owned, but operated and maintained by the Class 50 Alliance
Having been withdrawn due to relatively minor defects, 50031 was quickly put into service and worked its first trains in preservation on the SVR in May 1992. The Fifty Fund already owned 50035 and 50044 but also acted as custodians of the privately owned 50031. The additional arrival gave the group an operational '50' to represent it at heritage railway events.

When the ban on preserved diesel locomotives working on the national network was lifted in the 1990s, it was inevitable that a Class 50 would return to the mainline at some stage. The excellent condition of 50031 led to the Fifty Fund selecting it for recertification for mainline use and it duly worked the 'Pilgrim Hoover' for Past Time Railtours from Birmingham International to Plymouth and back on 1 November 1997.

The locomotive became a regular site on the mainline for the best part of a decade, including working timetabled service trains for Arriva Trains Wales (ATW). In January 2007, while working an empty stock train for ATW, 50031 suffered a main generator failure, leading to a long period out of service.

After being taken to LNWR at Crewe, 50031's power unit was removed for repair. This was refitted in early 2009, and the locomotive was later moved to Cardiff Canton depot for completion of repairs. June 2010 saw 50031 return to its home on the SVR, where it quickly re-entered service. It will not return to the mainline however, until it has had a full bogie overhaul and is fitted with replacement wheelsets.

Plans to repaint 50031 in the orange and white livery carried by the English Electric CP1800 locomotives based on the Class 50 and operating in Portugal, have been put on hold. For now, it remains painted in weather worn large logo livery. This represents the year 1990 when it worked in the DCWA pool of locomotives for departmental duties on the Western region of British Rail.

50033 *Glorious*
Owner: Swindon Borough Council (STEAM Museum) - in the care of 50021 Locomotive Association.
It was with surprise that many reacted to the National Railway

Museum's (NRM) announced intention to claim a Class 50 for the National Collection, as by then many had already been preserved. The chosen locomotive was 50033, which had survived a chequered period in the final years of the fleet to become one of Laira's final railtour trio.

Freshly repainted in large logo livery following bodywork attention at Laira, 50033 was driven into the NRM after working its final trains - a return trip from York to Scarborough on 20 March 1994. The locomotive was officially handed over at a ceremony on the first day of April.

Over the next few years 50033 paid several visits to heritage railways, but in spite of being part of the National Collection an announcement by the NRM in 2003 put its future in doubt. Following a review of the NRM's collection, it had been decided to de-register a number of exhibits and offer them for disposal - with 50033 being the most high profile. No sooner had the announcement been made, a number of existing '50' owners made representations to the NRM about taking the beleaguered 50033 on.

In spite of such offers, the NRM decided to transfer ownership of 50033 to Swindon Borough Council, who wished to display it at its STEAM museum - established in part of the former Swindon Works. At the time 50033 was on a working visit to the NYMR, and a series of farewell operating days were organised, with its last day in traffic being on 14 August 2004.

Soon afterwards, 50033 was moved to Swindon where it was put on display in one of the main halls in the museum. Its new owners suggested that 50033 may be able to visit heritage railways occasionally - but this did not placate those disappointed that a working '50' was going on indefinite static display. That said it was at least being stored undercover.

After less than three years at STEAM, it was announced that 50033 was to be loaned to RailSchool - a project being established in North Woolwich to train young people in engineering disciplines. The Class 50 was to be used as a training tool in the manner that the Operation Collingwood locomotives had been envisaged. Following this latest turn of events, 50033 was

First of the last

50049 *Defiance* spent the early years of its preservation career painted into its unique Railfreight triple grey livery as 50149. The locomotive is displayed at the Exeter Rail Fair in May 1994.

Andrew Fuller

moved to Tyseley Locomotive Works while planning for the RailSchool project was finalised.

RailSchool however, was never established and 50033 remained at Tyseley slowly deteriorating in open store. With much speculation as to its future, the locomotive was placed in the care of the 50021 Association - also based at Tyseley, who would start work to restore 50033 to working condition.

Following several years without use, the new custodians found the engine had seized. After some hard work however, the Association made good progress and by May 2010 the locomotive had made limited movements around the Tyseley Works complex - its first under its own power in six years. Perhaps a more stable future awaits 50033 after all!

50035 Ark Royal
Owner: Class 50 Alliance
50035 became the first Class 50 to be preserved, being handed over to the Fifty Fund at the Old Oak Common Open Day in August 1991 by Network SouthEast Managing Director Chris Green.

The locomotive was moved to St Leonard's depot for volunteers to begin the task of returning 50035 to working order, before moving

50039 *Implacable* was scrapped in July 1991 by Coopers Metals at Old Oak Common. The long-scrapped '50' was revived courtesy of 50042 *Triumph* on the Bodmin and Wenford Railway in Cornwall in May 2009 for a private charter.   **Martin Hart**

to the SVR in September 1996, where the Fifty Fund had decided to base the locomotive. 50035 went on to become a regular performer on the railway, but in late 2004 the locomotive developed a main generator failure and was moved to Old Oak Common for repairs and an overhaul.

In 2009, the closure of Old Oak Common due to the development of Crossrail, saw the nearly completed 50035 move to Eastleigh Works. Whilst at Old Oak, a start had been made on painting it into Loadhaul orange and black livery - a colour scheme never carried by a Class 50 and it was renumbered 50135.

The gleaming 50135 made its debut at the Eastleigh Works open weekend in May 2009, before stopping off at Long Marston for another open weekend on its way back to its SVR base. The '50' has now resumed its preserved working career and at the present time there are no plans to re-certify the '50' for main line use.

50040 Leviathan (scrapped)
Owner: Privately owned
The story of 50040 is similar to that of 50023, in that it was one of four '50s' bought from CF Booth scrapyard by the Operation Collingwood scheme, but was then sold on as a source of spares in 2001 and moved to the

Coventry Railway Centre.
By the time it was delivered to Coventry it was in a very poor condition, and after a few more years it changed owners again, being bought by HT as spare for 50008. Now deemed well beyond any form of restoration, once HT had recovered all the spares it wanted from 50040, the remains were sold to Paul Spracklen, the owner of 50026, for final spares recovery.

Having dodged the scrapman for more than 18 years, time finally ran out for 50040 in July 2008, when it was removed to Sims scrapyard in Halesowen and the remains were scrapped within days.

50042 Triumph
Owner: Bodmin and Wenford Diesel Group
50042 was withdrawn as surplus to requirements and was simply switched off when stood down by BR in October 1990. By the time it appeared for sale on a BR tender list however, a number of components had been either removed or stolen from 50042 and it had also suffered from some vandalism whilst in storage.

Purchased by the Bodmin and Wenford Diesel Group, it was moved to the Bodmin and Wenford Railway in March 1992, where work began almost immediately to return it to

A controversial decision in 2009 saw 50035 *Ark Royal* repainted into Loadhaul orange and black - a livery never carried by the class in BR days. The '50' also sports the number 50135. **Martin Hart**

use. Five months later, 50042 was started for the first time in preservation and it moved under its own power again in November 1992.

Following a repaint into large logo blue the locomotive settled down to become a reliable performer. During its time in preservation it has visited other heritage railways in the South West to take part in diesel events, including the P&DSR and the Dartmoor Railway.

In 2006, 50042 was taken out of service for general repairs and a bodywork overhaul and repaint into BR blue. Since returning to traffic in late 2006, 50042 has operated on a number of occasions disguised as various scrapped '50s'.

50043 *Eagle* (Scrapped)
Owner: Privately owned

50043 was withdrawn by BR following a main generator flashover and was bought as a source of spares by the 16SVT Society, which was restoring 40118 at Tyseley Locomotive Works. Although the 16SVT Society had no intention of restoring 50043 to working order, it was cosmetically restored and displayed at a number of open days, before it was returned to Tyseley for component recovery.

Once the 16SVT Society had recovered all the spares it wanted from 50043, the locomotive was sold to a private individual who intended to restore it to working order, and it moved to the P&BR, where 50029 and 50030 were also

stored by Operation Collingwood.

Restoration of the now heavily stripped 50043 was never going to be an easy task however, and in 2001 the owner decided not to proceed with its restoration. 50043 was another locomotive sold to the owner of 50026 who stripped it of any remaining spares before the remains were scrapped on site at the P&BR in January 2002.

50044 *Exeter*
Owner: Class 50 Alliance

50044 was bought by the Fifty Fund as its second locomotive, having been stored at Stratford, but it had not been as extensively robbed of spares as some of the other '50s'. One noticeable item missing was the number panel on one side, which had

First of the last

been cut out of the bodyside.

The newly acquired locomotive moved to St Leonard's depot to join 50035 and work began on restoring the '50' to working order. The new owners decided to cosmetically restore the locomotive to as-built condition, although the mechanical and electrical alterations done to the '50' at refurbishment would not be reversed.

The de-furbished 50044 emerged from St Leonard's in 1994 carrying rail blue and *Exeter* nameplates and crests, representing the period between April 1978 and when 50044 was shopped for refurbishment in late 1981.

After a period working on the SVR, the owners decided to certify D444 - as it was now known having lost its nameplates and multiple working equipment - for main line use, and the process of recertification began.

D444 returned to main line use in 1998 and was used on a number of occasions around South Wales with 50031, but suffered from main generator problems in 1999 and again in 2001. During its time out of traffic it was repainted into unauthentic two-tone green in a style similar to that of the Class 47s when they were first built in the early 1960s.

Although D444 has spent a lot of time out of traffic, it was recertified for main line use again in 2008 and is now fitted with mandatory OTMR and TPWS equipment.

50049 *Defiance*
Owner: Class 50 Alliance
The last-built Class 50 was purchased by the Class 50 Society, which became known as Project Defiance. Before leaving Laira depot, volunteers repainted it into Railfreight guise as 50149.

50149 moved to Allied Steel and Wire in Cardiff before moving to the WSR, where it remained until 1999 when it was relocated to the SVR to join the Fifty Fund locomotives based at the railway.

The close working relationship with the Fifty Fund saw 50049 registered for main line running, operating alongside 50031 and D444. This relationship was formalised in 2006, when the two organisations merged, becoming known as the Class 50 Alliance.

Since returning to main line use, 50049 has proved to be a consistent and reliable performer and, often accompanied by 50031 *Hood*, has travelled all around the country in a variety of liveries and on a whole host of routes that would not have been familiar to the Class 50s in BR days.

In 2009, at the end of almost a decade on the mainline, 50049 was taken out of service for a bogie and bodywork overhaul to take place. Once work is completed 50049 will return to main line service and will be painted into Large Logo blue livery with a black roof.

Number	Name	Normal Home Base	Status - Summer 2010
50002	*Superb*	South Devon Railway	Undergoing Restoration
50007	*Sir Edward Elgar*	Midland Railway Butterley	Operational
50008	*Thunderer*	Hanson Traction Washwood Heath	Operational
50015	*Valiant*	East Lancashire Railway	Operational
50017	*Royal Oak*	Plym Valley Railway	Operational
50019	*Ramillies*	Mid Norfolk Railway	Operational
50021	*Rodney*	Tyseley Locomotive Works	Undergoing Restoration
50026	*Indomitable*	Severn Valley Railway	Operational
50027	*Lion*	North Yorkshire Moors Railway	Operational
50029	*Renown*	Peak Rail	Stored
50030	*Repulse*	Peak Rail	Undergoing Restoration
50031	*Hood*	Severn Valley Railway	Operational
50033	*Glorious*	Tyseley Locomotive Works	Undergoing Restoration
50035	*Ark Royal*	Severn Valley Railway	Operational
50042	*Triumph*	Bodmin & Wenford Railway	Operational
50044	*Exeter*	Severn Valley Railway	Operational
50049	*Defiance*	Severn Valley Railway	Operational
50050	*Fearless*	Yeovil Railway Centre	Undergoing Restoration

It has often been argued that too many Class 50s were saved for preservation, and whilst three previously-preserved examples (including spares donor locomotive 50040) have been scrapped during the past few years, it has to be remembered than 32 of the fleet have now been scrapped.

The beginning of the end came in February 1987, when 50011 *Centurion* was withdrawn and sent to Crewe Works to act as a test-bed for overhauled Class 50 engines.

The next to succumb was 50006 *Neptune*, which was withdrawn in July 1987 - 50006 also subsequently gained the dubious distinction of being the first to be scrapped - at Vic Berry's yard in Leicester during March 1988.

Only one more Class 50 was withdrawn in 1987 - 50014 *Warspite* - but followers of the class now knew that the Class 50 was on borrowed time and further withdrawals would inevitably follow at an increasing rate.

A steady flow of withdrawals continued between 1988 and 1990, but by this stage BR was starting to make serious inroads into the fleet, and 1991 was the year when the most examples were stood down in the course of a single year.

By 1992, the fleet was down to just eight locomotives, with 50008 *Thunderer*, 50015 *Valiant*, 50029 *Renown*, 50030 *Repulse* and 50046 *Ajax* all withdrawn during the first half of the year. The withdrawal of these five left

just 50007 *Sir Edward Elgar*, 50033 *Glorious* and D400 in service - these locomotives being retained for railtours and special duties.

It is perhaps fitting that 50050 *Fearless* (D400) became one of the final two locomotives to be officially removed from BR's stock list, when it, along with 50007, was officially withdrawn on 31 March 1994.

Thankfully, the efforts of many preservationists across the country has ensured that the Class 50s live on, but we should remember those which are no longer with us. Over the next few pages we pay tribute to some of the locomotives which weren't lucky enough to survive the cutter's torch.

50014 *Warspite* was an early Class 50 casualty, being withdrawn in 1987 - one of the first three of the fleet to be stood down from active service. Pictured inside Laira depot a couple of days before official condemnation, 50014 has already lost its nameplates and other equipment as component recovery gets underway before disposal for scrap. *Peter Goodman*

First of the last

Above: 50011 *Centurion* was the first Class 50 to be withdrawn and it was moved to Crewe Works for testing overhauled power units. 50011 was scrapped in September 1992. *Martin Hart*

Left: 50025 *Invincible* failed to live up to its name when derailed by vandals at West Ealing in August 1989. It is being recovered from West Ealing in this image and was scrapped the following year at Old Oak Common. *Paul Winter*

Bottom: 50040 *Leviathan* was scrapped in 2008 after surviving for more than 18 years from its withdrawal. It is pictured waiting to be put out of its misery on 12 June 2005. *Martin Hart*

Overleaf Main Image: A line up Class 50s destined never to work again, all stand at a snow covered Old Oak Common facing the cutting torch. 50005 *Collingwood*, 50032 *Courageous* and 50034 *Furious* stand awaiting their fate.

Bottom Left: 50041 *Bulwark* was rebuilt after a major derailment in 1983, but its demise is close as it stands outside Old Oak Common's Factory along with 50024.

Bottom Right: 50039 *Implacable* poses in the sun at Old Oak Common. *All: Paul Winter*

Number	Withdrawn	Scrapped	Contractor & Location
50001	April 1991	December 2002	CF Booths, Rotherham
50003	July 1991	April 1992	MC Metals, Glasgow
50004	June 1990	May 1992	CF Booths, Rotherham
50005	January 1991	February 1991	Coopers Metals, Old Oak Common TMD
50006	July 1987	March 1988	Vic Berry, Leicester
50009	January 1991	February 1991	Coopers Metals, Old Oak Common TMD
50010	September 1988	May 1992	Coopers Metals, Plymouth Laira TMD
50011	February 1987	September 1992	Texas Metals, Crewe Works
50012	January 1989	July 1989	Vic Berry, Leicester
50013	March 1988	June 1989	Vic Berry, Leicester
50014	December 1987	July 1989	Vic Berry, Leicester
50016	August 1990	June 1992	CF Booths, Rotherham
50018	July 1991	June 1992	MC Metals, Glasgow
50020	July 1990	June 1992	CF Booths, Rotherham
50022	September 1988	June 1989	Vic Berry, Leicester
50023	October 1990	March 2004	Harry Needle Railroad Co, Barrow Hill
50024	February 1991	July 1991	Coopers Metals, Old Oak Common TMD
50025	August 1989	October 1989	Vic Berry, Old Oak Common TMD
50028	February 1991	July 1991	Coopers Metals, Old Oak Common TMD
50032	October 1990	February 1991	Coopers Metals, Old Oak Common TMD
50034	June 1990	February 1991	Coopers Metals, Old Oak Common TMD
50036	April 1991	July 1992	CF Booths, Rotherham
50037	September 1991	June 1992	MC Metals, Glasgow
50038	September 1988	June 1989	Vic Berry, Leicester
50039	June 1989	July 1991	Coopers Metals, Old Oak Common TMD
50040	November 1989	July 2008	Sims Metals, Halesowen
50041	April 1989	July 1991	Coopers Metals, Old Oak Common TMD
50043	February 1991	January 2002	Raxstar, Pontypool & Blaenavon Railway
50045	December 1990	April 2000	CF Booths, Rotherham
50046	June 1992	June 1992	MC Metals, Glasgow
50047	April 1988	May 1989	Vic Berry, Leicester
50048	July 1991	April 1992	MC Metals, Glasgow

First of the last

Above: Withdrawn 50023 *Howe* and 50019 *Ramillies* stand at the station end of Exeter Riverside yard awaiting disposal in March 1991. *Ian Horner*

Below: Following its derailment at West Ealing in August 1989, 50025 was taken to Old Oak Common, prior to its disposal. The severe extent of the damage is apparent in this view. *Hans Chowdhury*

First of the last

Above: 50024 *Vanguard* was withdrawn following a serious bogie fire, whilst working a West of England service, and some of the damage can be seen below the number panel. 50024 also gained non-standard NSE flashes in its headcode boxes at both ends of the locomotive - the only Class 50 to be so treated. *Paul Winter*

Below: 50010 *Monarch* was one of the early Class 50 withdrawals and was kept at Laira as a source of spares for the other '50s'. It was also the only Class 50 to be scrapped at the depot, being disposed of in May 1992. *Peter Goodman*

Number	Name	Named	De-named	Notes
50001	*Dreadnought*	10 April 1978	April 1991	
50002	*Superb*	21 March 1978	September 1991	Preserved un-named as D402.
50003	*Temeraire*	9 May 1978	July 1991	
50004	*St Vincent*	9 May 1978	June 1990	
50005	*Collingwood*	5 April 1978	January 1991	
50006	*Neptune*	25 September 1979	July 1987	
50007	*Hercules*	6 April 1978	February 1984	
	Sir Edward Elgar	25 February 1984		Preserved. Nameplates purchased by Class 40 Appeal with 50007. Replicas now carried.
50008	*Thunderer*	1 September 1978	May 1992	Preserved
50009	*Conqueror*	8 May 1978	January 1991	
50010	*Monarch*	16 March 1978	September 1988	
50011	*Centurion*	20 August 1979	February 1987	Nameplates transferred to 50040
50012	*Benbow*	3 April 1978	January 1989	
50013	*Agincourt*	19 April 1978	March 1988	
50014	*Warspite*	30 May 1978	December 1987	
50015	*Valiant*	21 April 1978	May 1992	Preserved
50016	*Barham*	3 April 1978	August 1990	
50017	*Royal Oak*	24 April 1978	September 1991	Preserved
50018	*Resolution*	6 April 1978	July 1991	
50019	*Ramillies*	18 April 1978	September 1990	Preserved
50020	*Revenge*	7 July 1978	July 1990	
50021	*Rodney*	31 July 1978	April 1990	Preserved
50022	*Anson*	20 April 1978	September 1988	
50023	*Howe*	17 May 1978	October 1990	
50024	*Vanguard*	15 May 1978	February 1991	
50025	*Invincible*	6 June 1978	August 1989	

Nameplate photographs: Paul Bettany, Matt Bradshaw, Peter Clay, Peter Goodman, Martin Hart, Ian Horner, Peter Horner, John Mah

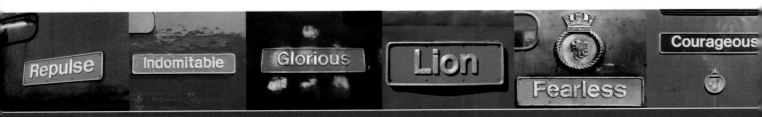

First of the last

Class 50 names

Number	Name	Named	De-named	Notes
50026	*Indomitable*	29 March 1978	December 1990	Preserved
50027	*Lion*	17 April 1978	July 1991	Preserved
50028	*Tiger*	10 May 1978	February 1991	
50029	*Renown*	14 November 1978	March 1992	Preserved
50030	*Repulse*	10 April 1978	April 1992	Preserved
50031	*Hood*	28 June 1978	August 1991	Preserved
50032	*Courageous*	17 July 1978	October 1990	
50033	*Glorious*	26 June 1978		Preserved. Nameplates presented to NRM with locomotive in March 1994
50034	*Furious*	6 April 1978	June 1990	
50035	*Ark Royal*	17 January 1978	August 1980	Preserved
50036	*Victorious*	16 May 1978	April 1991	
50037	*Illustrious*	8 June 1978	September 1991	
50038	*Formidable*	5 May 1978	September 1988	
50039	*Implacable*	20 June 1978	June 1989	
50040	*Leviathan*	15 September 1978	June 1987	
	Centurion	4 July 1987	November 1989	Nameplates transferred from 50040
50041	*Bulwark*	8 May 1978	April 1990	
50042	*Triumph*	4 October 1978	October 1990	Preserved
50043	*Eagle*	28 June 1978	February 1991	
50044	*Exeter*	27 April 1978	January 1991	Preserved. Different style now applied
50045	*Achilles*	12 April 1978	December 1990	
50046	*Ajax*	11 October 1978	March 1992	
50047	*Swiftsure*	26 May 1978	April 1988	
50048	*Dauntless*	16 March 1978	July 1991	
50049	*Defiance*	2 May 1978	August 1991	Preserved
50050	*Fearless*	4 August 1978 23 August 1978	7 August 1978 March 1994	Preserved. Plates removed March 1991 to March 1994 whilst painted as D400.

Background Nameplate Images: Peter Goodman

The life & times of 50050 *Fearless*

SUBSCRIBE TODAY
and receive 14 issues for the price of 12

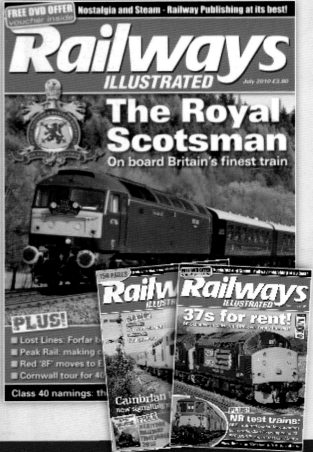

GREAT SUBSCRIBER BENEFITS

- Subscribe for only £11.40 by quarterly Direct Debit

- Receive each issue 'hot off the press' before the shops

- Convenient home delivery so that you never miss an issue

- **FREE** membership to the Ian Allan Publishing Subs Club

- **FREE** personalised Subscription Loyalty Card

- **EXCLUSIVE** access to new online site with great subscriber benefits, offers and competitions.
  Visit www.ianallanmagazines.com/subsclub for more details

FOR EASY PAYMENT USE OUR QUARTERLY DIRECT DEBIT OPTION - JUST £11.40 PER QUARTER!

CALL +44 (0)1932 266622

QUOTE CODE RI14 TO SUBSCRIBE TODAY! Offer valid until 05.08.10 and open to new subscribers only.

I would like to subscribe to *Railways Illustrated*, starting with the .... issue.

- ☐ 12 issues UK + 2 FREE ISSUES - £45.60
- ☐ 12 issues Europe + 2 FREE ISSUES - £55.20
- ☐ 12 issues ROW + 2 FREE ISSUES - £60.40
- ☐ Quarterly Direct Debit - £11.40 per quarter (UK only)

Your Details

Mr/Mrs/Miss/Ms: .... Forename: ....
Surname: ....
Address: ....
Post Code: .... Country: ....
Tel No: ....
Email: ....

Debit / Credit Card

Please debit my card for the amount £ ....
☐ Mastercard   ☐ Visa   ☐ Switch / Maestro Card
Card Number: ....
Exp date: .... Start date: .... Issue No: ....

Cardholders signature: .... Date: ....

Cheque

I enclose a cheque to the value of £ ....
(please make cheque payable to Ian Allan Publishing Ltd - Eurocheques are not accepted)

Direct Debit Form

Name of Bank / Building Society: ....
Address of Bank / Building Society: ....
.... Post Code: ....
Name of account holder: ....
Bank / Building Society Account Number: .... Branch Sort Code: ....

Service Users Number: 624943   Ref No. (office use only) ....
Instruction to your Bank or Building Society: Please pay Ian Allan Publishing Ltd Direct Debits from the account detailed in this Instruction subject to the safeguards assured by the Direct Debit Guarantee. I understand that this Instruction may remain with Ian Allan Publishing Ltd and, if so, details will be passed electronically to my Bank/Building Society.

Signature: .... Date: ....

The Direct Debit Guarantee
- This Guarantee is offered by all banks and building societies that accept instructions to pay Direct Debits.
- If there are any changes to the amount, date or frequency of your Direct Debit Ian Allan Publishing Ltd will notify you 10 working days in advance of your account being debited or as otherwise agreed. If you request Ian Allan Publishing Ltd to collect a payment, confirmation of the amount and date will be given to you at the time of the request.
- If an error is made in the payment of your Direct Debit, by Ian Allan Publishing Ltd or your bank or building society you are entitled to a full and immediate refund of the amount paid from your bank or building society.
  — If you receive a refund you are not entitled to, you must pay it back when Ian Allan Publishing Ltd asks you to.
- You can cancel a Direct Debit at any time by simply contacting your bank or building society. Written confirmation may be required. Please also notify us.

Please complete and send to: *Railways Illustrated* Subscriptions, Ian Allan Publishing Ltd, Riverdene Business Park, Molesey Road, Hersham, Surrey KT12 4RG.

Tel: +44 (0)1932 266622 ■ Fax: +44 (0)1932 266633 ■ subs@ianallanpublishing.co.uk

Offer ends 05.08.10. Only open to new subscribers. Code RI14

From time to time, Ian Allan Publishing may contact you with information or offers regarding subscriptions and other products. If you do not wish to receive such information or offers, then please tick the following box ☐